Praise for *Say Yes*

"It is undeniably true tha[...] society and every type of relationship; marriage, special commitments, friendships, personal feelings of self-worth, and our connections with God or Higher Power. It is also the source of toxic guilt and shame.

"Sexual addiction reveals itself in a variety of behaviors: internet porn, adultery, voyeurism, phone sex, and compulsive use of pornography . . . to name a few.

"Where does it come from? Well, like other addictions it is the result of *emotional brokenness* that affects the body, mind, and spirit. The goal of treatment and healing is to develop, over a period of time, a healthy expression of sexuality; this often includes therapy, meditation, and prayer.

"Rev. Leo Booth, with his experience of counseling sex addicts for many years, is reflecting his insights in this powerful book *Say Yes to Your Sexual Healing*, where he boldly addresses what sex addicts must face in order to recover.

"This book offers gentle and nonjudgmental meditations for healing and recovery. I strongly recommend *Say Yes to Your Sexual Healing* for sex addicts, their families, and friends."
                                    —Jess Montgomery, M.D.,
                        medical director/Santé Center for Healing

"I enjoy and appreciate Rev. Leo's spiritual wisdom into sexual addiction; his insights will help many."
                                    —Ron Arrington, M.S., LCDC,
                        clinical director/Santé Center for Healing

"Rev. Leo Booth's nurturing and encouraging meditations will help those afflicted with sexual addiction live 'one day at a time' in their pursuit of growth and healing. Each meditation provides a daily message of inspiration and hope that is so important to recovery."

—Stephanie Carnes, Ph.D.

"*Say Yes to Your Sexual Healing* is a very worthwhile tool for everyone in the sex addiction world. Rev. Leo Booth speaks from his heart to our hearts with clarity, pathos, and at times humor. It is a practical book which I shall recommend to our patients at Psychological Counseling Services."

—Ralph H. Earle, M.Div., Ph.D.

Also by Leo Booth

Say Yes to Your Spirit
Say Yes to Your Life

SAY YES TO YOUR

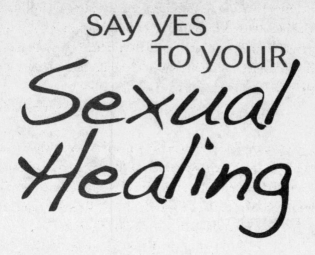

Sexual
Healing

DAILY MEDITATIONS FOR
OVERCOMING SEX ADDICTION

LEO BOOTH

Health Communications, Inc.
Deerfield Beach, Florida

www.hcibooks.com

Library of Congress Cataloging-in-Publication Data

Booth, Leo, 1946-
  Say yes to your sexual healing : daily meditations for overcoming sex
addiction / Leo Booth.
      p. cm.
   ISBN-13: 978-0-7573-1378-3 (trade paper)
   ISBN-10: 0-7573-1378-7 (trade paper)
   1. Sex addicts—Meditations.   2. Sexual addiction—Meditations
3. Compulsive behavior—Meditations.   4. Devotional calendars.
I. Title.
   BL625.9.S49.B66 2009
   204'.32—dc22

                                                          2009002914

© 2009 Leo Booth

All rights reserved. Printed in the United States of America. No part of this
publication may be reproduced, stored in a retrieval system, or transmitted
in any form or by any means, electronic, mechanical, photocopying, record-
ing, or otherwise, without the written permission of the publisher.

HCI, its logos, and marks are trademarks of Health Communications, Inc.

Publisher: Health Communications, Inc.
          3201 S.W. 15th Street
          Deerfield Beach, FL 33442-8190

Cover design by Larissa Hise Henoch
Interior design by Lawna Patterson Oldfield

In the early 1990s I started an inpatient program for sex addiction in Southern California. Soon I heard of a recovery service on Sunday mornings that our patients could attend. Some went to see what it was about and came back awed. The service, they reported, was inspiring and helpful, and it integrated the 12 Steps. Soon most of the patients would go no matter what their faith of origin. The Episcopal priest who led the services was warm, funny, and insightful. Most important from a patient's point of view, he seemed to understand and appreciate the difficulties of sex addiction recovery. Early recovery for sex addicts presents many spiritual challenges, and this service helped many start the sorting process most have to confront at that stage. Sundays in inpatient settings tend to be off days. But gratefully for our patients, Sunday was one of the week's high points.

That is how I came to know Rev. Leo Booth. His reputation preceded him, and I learned it was well deserved. I have watched audiences enjoy his wit and his abilities. I know how his writing has helped many. And I have witnessed what many do not know. He has extended himself to help others in ways that can only be described as "service." In 12 Step tradition, "service" has an important nuance. This is where you do the work to help out, like everyone else, without the expectation of being noticed or recognized. Plus he is one of those who have had the courage to reach out to those whose struggles extend into the realm of human sexuality. In many ways this book is the natural extension of these themes I have come to know about in Rev. Leo's life.

And that fits the purpose of the work in which you as a reader are about to engage. Our task is to move from obsession into focus. Our very neurobiology requires that we have the humility to realize that it is an everyday effort. So if you wish to make a sexual shift in your life, you start with the basic humility that everyone has the struggle. No pill, no profound insight, and no quick formula will reengineer your sexual neural circuitry. Only concentrated effort does it. Every day presents its sexual challenges. How we respond is the medium by which we change how our brain works.

It is one of our most important tasks. The brain categorizes sexual stimuli 20 percent faster than any other stimulation we have been able to measure. It is one of the fastest nonchemical ways we have to access the pleasure centers of the brain. Our species is wired for sexual intensity because it was a matter of survival. When that goes awry, it creates a world of hurt. As a reader who acquired this book, you probably already know that part. Even more important is that our sexual decisions shape culture. Research shows that violence, mental health, attachment to others, and the ability to raise emotionally healthy children all start with how men and women treat each other sexually. Sometimes we lose sight of that as we sort through our own sexual labyrinth. It is more than just you. Each of us adds to our culture and species with each decision, every day.

So this book in many ways is a guide to those daily encounters that individually and together are so important. But it is also a journey with a very experienced, helpful guide, whose humor and wisdom keep us focused. Like all of these journeys, there will be difficult moments. But as the days accumulate, gratitude will emerge. Your focus will create new sexual realities and a better life.

—*Patrick J. Carnes, Ph.D.*

Introduction

When Leo Booth called to say he was writing a book called *Say Yes to Your Sexual Healing*, I immediately went back to a meditation he had written, "My Name Is Shame," in *Meditations for Compulsive People*.

With his permission, I have used and adapted this meditation in several lectures, and I've always considered it nothing less than genius. Leo entered the world of shame in a new and insightful way, touching not only upon sexual abuse but upon a religious rigidity that forced shame into the shadows.

His new meditation book, *Say Yes to Your Sexual Healing*, is even more profound. This book gives testimony to the hundreds of men and women who trusted his wisdom and shared their stories, knowing their words were safe with him and yet would be used to help and heal others. The actual quotations from sex addicts he's counseled are masterful, and he takes the reader *immediately* into the sickness—and into the toxic shame. Many meditation books touch gently upon the topic they are dealing with—not *Say Yes to Your Sexual Healing*. Leo confronts sex addiction as it truly is, in all its manifestations, and nothing is spared.

We read about the covert behavior created by unhealthy religious teachings that have implied that all things sexual are nasty—indeed that sex itself is sinful—and about millions who have hidden in shame-based hypocrisy, saying one thing while living another.

We read about inappropriate sexual behavior with family members, some of them children, and Leo handles the spiritual message with gentleness alongside the requirement for responsible therapy. Pedophiles are not excused, but neither are they bludgeoned to death. His approach to spirituality breathes into the darkest corners of sexual misconduct, bringing hope and healing.

Leo gives helpful advice to the people who are often called *sex addict, sexual compulsive,* or *sexual anorexic.* He clearly explains how these descriptions might be understood. He is most insightful when it comes to their pathological complexities.

This precious book is written by a spiritual master. It provides a healing read for sex addicts and their families, as well as an educational read for professionals seeking a spiritual therapy for treating this "cunning, baffling, and powerful" disease. Dare I say it? *This book is a must-read for everyone.*

John Bradshaw

Acknowledgments

When writing a book you come to value the friends and colleagues you have around you. This book, *Say Yes to Your Sexual Healing*, is the creation of many valuable minds, many comments I've heard along the way, very many discussions over coffee until late into the night. As always, some people stand out.

Kien Lam supported the initial concept and added ideas while he edited my very early manuscript. He's been my office manager for many years and is my most cherished mentor.

Hilary Fitzsimmons and Michael Schultheis, who work in my office, read and typed the manuscripts, again presenting improvements that have enhanced the book.

Michele Matrisciani, who is an executive editor at Health Communications, Inc., worked tirelessly to improve the writing and tighten up my thoughts, making *Say Yes to Your Sexual Healing* vivid and clear.

Gary Seidler, who planted the seed, is a trusted friend. I know that more will be developed from having his professional vision.

Patrick Carnes kindly wrote the foreword for this book

and allowed me to develop new spiritual concepts with the patients at his facility.

John Bradshaw, an old friend, also took time out from a busy schedule to write a much appreciated introduction.

I also appreciated the feedback and endorsements from Jess Montgomery, Ron Arrington, Ralph M. Earle, and Stephanie Carnes.

Peter Vegso, publisher at Health Communications, Inc., said "Yes" immediately to the initial concept of this book and made it happen.

Have I left people out? Yes. Forgive me and please know that you are not forgotten in my feelings of gratitude.

Author's Note

For a number of years, I've been working as a spiritual consultant to some treatment centers that address sexual compulsivity, particularly the Sante Center for Healing in Denton, Texas.

For the past ten years, the conversation concerning sexual compulsivity has dramatically increased, and what used to be accompanied by an embarrassing laugh is now seriously accepted as an addiction and a gateway behavior to alcohol and drug relapse. Those of us who are in recovery from alcoholism should not be surprised.

In the groundbreaking book *Alcoholics Anonymous* (first published in 1939), Bill Wilson stated his belief that sexual compulsions were a serious issue for alcoholics to consider:

> Now about sex. Many of us needed an overhauling there. But above all, we tried to be sensible on this question. It's so easy to get off track. Here we find human opinions running to extremes—absurd extremes, perhaps. One set of voices cry that sex is a lust of our lower nature, a base necessity of procreation. Then we have the voices who cry for sex and more sex; who bewail the institution of marriage; who think that most of the

troubles of the race are traceable to sex causes. They think we do not have enough of it, or that it isn't the right kind. They see its significance everywhere. One school would allow man no flavor for his fare and the other would have us all on a straight pepper diet. We want to stay out of this controversy. We do not want to be the arbiter of anyone's sex conduct. *We all have sex problems. We'd hardly be human if we didn't. What can we do about them?* (emphasis added) (p. 68)

Bill Wilson also felt, in certain situations, that counseling might be appropriate:

Counsel with persons is often desirable, but we let God be the final judge. We realize that some people *are as fanatical about sex as others are loose. We avoid hysterical thinking or advice.* (emphasis added) (p. 69)

And then comes a dire warning:

If we are not sorry, and our conduct continues to harm others, we are quite sure to drink. We are not theorizing. These are facts out of experience.

I had directly addressed sexual compulsivity and "secret sex" some years ago when I wrote *When God Becomes a Drug*. It was clear to me then that a repressive religious atmosphere forced the sexual behavior of many churchgoers and Bible Christians into secrecy, creating a covert constellation of hidden and shameful behaviors. This religious "denial" became a fertile ground for sexual compulsivity. The belief that sex is dirty creates intense shame about our very being. It fuels the belief that our bodies and any kind of physical pleasure are dirty; thus it fosters extreme self-hate and confusion about the sources of pleasure and can lead to such abuses as anorexia, self-flagellation, or self-mutilation. Incest survivors in particular are vulnerable to these forms of self-abuse; the idea that sex is dirty fuels their belief that they caused the abuse, so they take their shame out on their bodies, sometimes burning or cutting or trying to starve themselves.

This particular symptom of religious abuse fuels the belief that we are mistakes, garbage, depraved. I believe that God created sex and made it pleasurable to us for a reason: not just to procreate but as a means of physically expressing spiritual unity. To insist that it is dirty is an abuse of God's gift, and from that abuse springs more abuse, guilt, shame, humiliation, fear.

In *When God Becomes a Drug*, I also wrote that this conflict often produces the dual diseases of religious addiction and sex addiction. The dogma about the evils of the flesh— teachings that state only whores enjoy sex and that love is not nurturing but angry and condemning—conflicts with the human desire for closeness. James Wall, who wrote an article about the Jimmy Swaggart sex scandal, noted, "I have read that an interest in pornography stems from an intense loneliness. A longing for intimacy is basic to us all. Most of us don't turn to pornography to meet that need, but we all have our ways" ("Swaggart's Confession: There's Room to

Mourn," *Christian Century*, March 1988). Wall has correctly identified some of the core issues of religious addiction: loneliness, anger, and shame, resulting in a distance from other people and God.

In my work as a spiritual consultant to people in treatment centers, I have had numerous meetings and consultations with sex addicts, their families, and their friends. I've also listened attentively to therapists, psychiatrists, and psychologists talk about the tragic stories of unaddressed sex addiction, and I've created this daily meditation book from my notes and the actual comments of many sex addicts.

You do not have to know sexually compulsive people or listen to their therapists to be aware of the fact that sex addiction, or the notion that our society has become sexually unbalanced, is widespread:

- Almost every hotel and motel in the United States offers "adult movie" rentals, which are not listed as such at checkout.
- Network and cable television channels are becoming increasingly more "adult" in content, with a dramatic shift toward sexually explicit language and nudity.
- The Internet has created a billion-dollar business with various pornographic websites meeting every proclivity.

Sex sells. It always has—only today it has a younger and greater audience. Also, thanks to the brilliance of technology, it can be brought into your home comfortably and anonymously.

You don't need to be a sex addict or sexual compulsive to be challenged every day by the blatant invasion of sexually explicit material. As I have said, sex is everywhere, and it is used to sell almost everything—dolls to dusters! We are all affected by this.

Hence the need for this little book, which brings a healthy spiritual balance to the topic of sexuality. I wrote it with the sexually compulsive in mind, but it also conveys a message of hope to family and friends. Indeed, when we consider that sexual energy is a gift from God and yet it has been the source of abuse and temptation from the beginning of time, it would seem only common sense to place sexuality within the context of living the spiritual life.

Is this book for all sex addicts? Well, it can only help the people who truly want help. There are undeniably some alcoholics who make the choice, as a balanced decision, to continue to drink . . . and yes, there are some addicts who are unrepentant, repeat offenders, who probably have other mental health issues and are unable or unwilling to give up their abusive sexual behavior. This book will not help them. However, they are a tragic few; the vast majority of sex addicts will find this book both helpful and hopeful.

I trust you will find *Say Yes to Your Sexual Healing* both challenging and helpful.

Rev. Leo Booth

Hope

I've celebrated one year in Sex Addicts Anonymous. It has been the best year of my life, and my marriage is slowly getting back on track.

We can celebrate the first of the year knowing that people are recovering from sex addiction one day at a time. As with alcoholics and addicts, families are coming together, relationships are healing, and people are slowly picking up the broken pieces and beginning to live again.

We can dwell on those who are not getting help, but today is a time to celebrate the spiritual program that is helping to cultivate positive and creative human beings.

I believe in the "Say Yes to Your Life" principle: If we choose, we may overcome most of the challenges that face us. Yes, we will certainly need help, but these helpers are also helped, and we all become a healing fellowship.

Today I continue to say "Yes"
to my recovery.

Balance

Sex is like anything else: It can be valued or abused.

Spiritually, we know that anything can be abused: food, alcohol, work, prescription drugs. . . . The list goes on and on, and sex is no different.

When we speak about sex addiction, we are talking about a compulsive behavior that distorts who we are, distorts other people, and, if left untreated, can destroy any family or relationship.

A therapist said to me recently that you are open to abuse if you make a gift less or more than it was meant to be. It is in this sense that sex becomes abusive. It is an ingredient of love, affection, and friendship. However, it was never intended to stand alone.

I appreciate my sexuality in
the context of love.

Obsession

I'm impotent, but I still obsess about pornography.

When we hear about sex addiction, we often think that the addict is a sexual athlete, having sex perhaps four or more times a day, with a potency that is enormous.

However, I have heard the preceding quotation many times. The individual often does not get an erection but is mentally compulsive about seeing sex around him. He becomes the codependent giver of pleasure, obsessed with the "thought" of sex.

This person is so out of balance with the nature of a healthy sexual relationship that he often cannot see how his obsession concerning sex is destroying any intimacy he might have attained.

With his loved ones, even the stranger, he becomes scary, abusive, and almost fanatical.

I pray for a balanced sexuality.

Compulsion

Nothing is more important to me than sex. If the chemistry is there, I cannot resist.

"I cannot resist." This phrase is often used in connection with addiction and compulsive behavior.

- I can't resist alcohol.
- If food is around, I can't resist it.
- I know the heroin is killing me, but I can't resist it.

The language for the sex addict, when listened to carefully, is the same as the words used by other addicts. That gives us hope.

The challenge, for all of us, is to begin the conversation concerning sex addiction in our society and to be willing to uncover any obstacles that hinder our path: family, religion, etiquette, social or cultural impediments.

*I seek courage in facing
my sex addiction.*

Unmanageable

Yesterday I "flashed" some girl on the freeway.
My life is becoming increasingly unmanageable.

The First Step of Alcoholics Anonymous is "We admitted we were powerless over alcohol—that our lives had become unmanageable."

Addiction will eventually take us into the danger zone. For people who do not have an addiction issue, and I believe they are few in number when you consider the many addictions in contemporary society, it is difficult to believe that addicts would do what they do. That's why addicts often describe themselves (poetically) as insane: "The things I know I should not do are the things I want to do!" (St. Paul's letter to Romans 7:15)

Desperation will eventually create disaster: divorce, bankruptcy, prison, or death.

Thank you for the 12 Step program.

Masturbation

I began masturbating when I was nine or ten. I'm thirty, and I masturbate five to ten times a day. It's a problem.

Compulsive behavior: It is less unsettling when it concerns chocolate, bingo, shopping, or work, but when it comes to sex, particularly *masturbation*, many people do not want to face it or talk about it.

Let's be honest. We don't talk about some things in our society. Some things are not "nice." Some things are considered better left unsaid. And the world becomes a sicker place.

This certainly seems to be true in the area of sexuality. Pornography is on the increase. Child sexual abuse cases seem to be in the news on a weekly, if not daily, basis. Sexual crimes are at an all-time high—and yet some people still wish to turn away.

Denial is no longer an option. Sex addiction is real and here to stay, and compulsive masturbation is only one aspect of this problem.

I will begin to talk about my sexual issues.

Fantasy

*Sometimes I wish that God had not created sex.
The wish doesn't last long!*

This was said to me recently by a woman who was in treatment for alcoholism and sexual compulsivity. I remember her smile after she had made that remark—thank God for humor.

I know, however, what she was feeling. Sometimes we wish we did not have the behaviors that make us human beings because, if abused or enthusiastically pursued, these behaviors can bring enormous pain. A gift can become a curse.

Well, let's not get too dramatic; it depends how we use or cherish the gift. Sex addiction demonstrates a lack of balance, feelings of powerlessness, and, like any compulsion, it can be treated. Sufferers are healed. As Jesus remarked, "Physician, heal thyself." (Luke 4:23)

*I'm grateful for the power
to change my life.*

Understanding

My mind can sometimes be obsessed with sexual thoughts. Everyone becomes a sexual object, even my young children.

In therapy it is often said that "You are only as sick as your secrets." Only when you can talk about your secrets will you heal.

I believe this to be true, but the listener must be prepared to hear what the secrets are about—and that's not always comfortable. A person who talks about sexually objectifying his own children disturbs many people.

To understand sex addiction, a person must be spiritually strong and recognize that the essential human being is different from the behavior. The sex addict or abuser was often the victim of abuse. He or she was once a young child looking for love and nurture—only to be damaged by abuse.

I seek to discover the divine spark in everyone I meet.

Denial

I caught my son having sex with his girlfriend.
I said nothing. To this day I've said nothing.
But I think about it every day. Why can't I talk
about it?

Shame is a strange feeling. It can create denial, secrecy, and isolation. For many people, sex is surrounded by shame. Indeed, sex often lives within the shame.

What we see we deny, what happened we ignore, what we are doing we minimize—while always seeking to protect the veneer of normality.

From this arises the need for sexual healing and treatment. We can begin to examine where our shame comes from and to slowly create a healthy message by which to live.

I seek a spirituality that enables me
to live in the world of reality.

Compassion

I heard about a woman who had sex with her dog. I came home and tried it. Now I feel so guilty and ashamed.

When we talk about sex addiction, we often make reference to the First Step of Alcoholics Anonymous: *We admitted we were powerless over alcohol—that our lives had become unmanageable.*

But the words *powerless* and *unmanageable* do not do justice to the guilt and shame, or to that place of spiritual degradation that a person can reach. What must the feelings be like for a person who has had sex with an animal?

For some people, their shadow is really dark. And yet I understand. Sick people do sick things.

The spiritual component for treating an addict involves compassion, understanding, and the belief that they can heal.

*My spiritual program is
based upon compassion.*

Sex

God is love. But what about sex?

God's love involves sex. So many words are used to express love: *romance, passion, creativity, interdependence, kindness, respect*—and our sexuality plays a role in manifesting them all.

I believe that we were created to create, and this involves the sexual ingredient that exists in all of us. Religious abuse affirmed that "divine love" could only be reached if we escaped our physical bodies. Celibacy and virginity were held up as examples of a "higher love," and many people became rigid, cold, judgmental, and passionless in their endeavors to reach this spiritual state.

Healthy sexuality takes us into the heart of God's creativity.

*My sexuality enables
me to love.*

Slippery Slope

I always wanted to have sex with two women. Soon it grew to be men and women. I was drowning in shame.

It started with a beer. Then I moved to beer and wine. Soon cocktails helped close the evening—and it was not long before I was drinking everything and anything!

That's my journey into alcoholism. Sex addiction is not exactly the same, but it is similar. The sex addict keeps lowering the bar. The end result for many is experiencing the same powerlessness and unmanageability. Families get destroyed. Relationships are lost. Our employment, issues with the law, and our personal health can all, eventually, be affected.

But the hope and recovery many alcoholics are experiencing today is also available to the sex addict.

Only when we are able to admit that a problem exists can healing and recovery begin: Step One!

I admit that my sex addiction is creating powerlessness.

Responsibility

I don't take sex seriously. It's like eating food.
Love only complicates things.

We live in a world that has different attitudes and beliefs about almost everything, including sex. Certainly many people hold the view that "sex is sex and food is food, so let's not make it complicated."

But it *is* complicated for many people. And it gets complicated because *feelings* are involved: anger, fear, jealousy, abandonment, and a sense of being used. My experience has been that sex addicts don't want to take their destructive behaviors seriously until they directly affect them.

It is undoubtedly true that love often involves sex. It needn't do so, but it usually does. The reality is that we have received many unhelpful messages from a variety of sources concerning sex and love.

Some things are complicated because they are!

Today I take sex seriously.

Abstinence

I'm seeking to heal my sexual compulsivity—
but I'm not wanting to be a monk!

In the treatment of sexual compulsivity, it is important to remember that the answer isn't to be *permanently* abstinent.

Food addicts must eat; work addicts still must work; and yes, sex addicts must have sexual expression. Celibacy is a choice, in reality, that few will make.

That does not mean that, with support and therapy, a sex addict might not accept a period of *healing abstinence*. How long might that be? Well, it will vary from person to person: six months, a year, three years, sometimes longer. That decision can only be made voluntarily between the therapist and the sex addict.

Today I commit to seeking
balance in my life that will involve
a period of sexual abstinence.

Self-Respect

*I can identify with love addiction. I often had
sex when I felt lonely and what I really wanted
was love.*

I see loneliness everywhere. Indeed, I experience it in
my own life. I often can go for weeks without seeing
a neighbor. Rarely do I have friends over for dinner. I
often make telephone calls just to hear a voice. I'm not
just alone—I'm lonely.

I heard an expression some years ago: "I'm skin
starved"—starved for human contact, hugs, intimacy,
and imprisoned in loneliness.

It is loneliness that helped create the love addiction.
To experience love, a person is willing to do anything,
even to provide sex.

*Today I know that I will remain
lonely until I begin to love
and respect myself.*

Relapse

*I was in a treatment center for alcoholism.
And all I wanted to do was have sex with the
girls. I relapsed on my way home.*

I've sensed for years as a consultant to treatment centers for addictions that many alcoholics had a sex addiction that was as serious, or *more* serious, than their alcoholism and drug dependency. It was their core addiction, their prime addiction, and in most cases it was never treated. Indeed, sex addiction was never discussed during treatment. Naturally, the patient continued to relapse.

I've heard people say that we must treat first things first. Well, sex addiction *is first* for some people, but if it's not discussed, not mentioned in treatment, ignored in the face of abusers acting out sexually, then people will continue to relapse.

The writing is clearly on the wall. Let's not ignore it.

*My continued relapse is connected
to my sex addiction.*

Guilt

I love sex. I think about sex all the time. It has become an obsession.

When I see the words "It has become an obsession" on paper, it cannot convey the expression on people's faces, the pain heard in their voice, or the awkwardness of their posture. Sex addiction is as damaging as any other addiction, and it is harder to discuss in therapy because of the shame and guilt.

With its constant emphasis on sex being a sin, religion has a role to play in the shame and guilt that sex addicts experience—and in the shame and guilt experienced by sex addicts' families and friends.

For the most part, we are not comfortable discussing sex in this society. Certain sexual behaviors are hard to verbalize. Anything that reveals the abuse of children produces anger, if not rage: *Sin* seems a more appropriate word than *sickness*. And while the religious clamor and moral confusion take center stage, the disease quietly slips out the door.

Today I affirm that the sex addict is sick, not sinful.

19

Isolation

My sexual activity isolates me.

For many years I've said at conferences that my definition of spirituality is "being a positive and creative human being." I came to this definition because as a drinking alcoholic I was both negative and destructive. I also felt isolated . . . misunderstood . . . alone.

I believe this is also true for the sex addict. At times we will find that therapists and psychiatrists will seek a variety of words to capture who the sex addict is: *covert, shamed, secretive, manipulative, seductive, insecure*—and yes, *isolated*.

Recovery, in this sense, must be poetic. Different words will resonate with the sex addict at different times because the disease is "cunning, baffling, and powerful." No one word or theory can capture its essence.

I am comprehensive in
my treatment of sex addiction.

Treatment

I asked God to remove my sexual compulsivity.
He didn't. So I continued. Now I have serious
legal problems.

God is not codependent. God is not about to fix or remove all our problems. We are not puppets on a string awaiting God's direction. Such a theology is an abuse of God!

I believe that we are responsible spiritually for our lives. I'm an alcoholic, and so I needed to ask for help some years ago. Then I went into treatment, actively pursued recovery, and today I take responsibility for my alcoholism—one day at a time. I prayed, but I also moved my feet.

The sex addict is no different. Yes, many people do not accept or understand sex addiction, but some understand it and are able to create healing. The sex addict must find these people and ask for help.

God is on the side of therapy, not excuses.

I affirm my responsibility
for my health.

Sin

I was told that sex was the worst sin. It was so bad that nice people didn't even talk about it.

In this statement we see the serious challenge in the treatment and healing of sex addicts: People are fearful to talk about it.

Most people who are reading this meditation grew up in families that did not talk about sex. Indeed, when sex was talked about it usually came in the form of a joke.

I believe that the gift of sex is spiritual: It enables people to express love in a tangible and satisfying way. However, compulsive sex tarnishes the gift and can easily destroy a loving relationship.

Spiritually, we must bring sex out of the shadows and treat the sex addict and his or her significant relationships respectfully. Regardless of the shame that many of us carry concerning our sexual expression, we must affirm clearly that *sex is not a sin*.

I seek to respect the gift of sexuality.

Temptation

As a child I grew up hearing profanity. Today my favorite words are profane.

W hen I was young I was perversely attracted to what I was told not to do, and I got a childish pleasure in shocking my friends with words my parents told me were "bad" or "naughty."

When I have counseled addicts who were attracted to the edge, those who loved to push the envelope, I could always identify with them. We have all heard stories of addicts and alcoholics who were inevitably seduced into a danger zone. Well, this is also true for sex addicts.

A captivating high, an adrenaline rush, was found in the forbidden: in the forbidden touch, in watching videos that could send you to hell, in saying the crudest of words.

I understand that small beginnings
can have tragic endings.

Objectifying

I found girlie magazines in my father's bag.
That was about the time that I began looking
at women as sexual objects.

I've heard similar statements from patients being treated for sex addiction, and I believe it is true for millions of men who never receive treatment.

In my talks on spirituality, I've said that human beings imitate: We imitate language, fashion, behavior. Our parents play a major role in this behavior.

A father can have a powerful influence on his son—"The apple does not fall far from the tree." A father's objectification of women is passed on to the son, which can develop into sex addiction.

When we begin to share our childhood stories, we discover others who can identify, and we are not alone. Only when we can see and talk about our past are we able to heal from it.

I am ready to share.

Gayness

I am gay, and I am ashamed of some of the things I have done.

A friend of mine thought his sex addiction was an aspect of his being gay. After therapy he realized that this was not true. Yes, his loneliness and secrecy concerning his sexual activity as a teenager led him to seek sex compulsively in parks and public restrooms. The shame created by his anonymous sexual escapades led to guilt and an even greater feeling of unworthiness, which eventually took him back to the parks and restrooms.

However, when he entered therapy he was directed to support groups and slowly began to have meaningful relationships as a gay man. He discovered a spiritual expression of his love, and he has now been in a healthy relationship for ten years.

He's not perfect. Occasionally he gets lonely. But he's happy.

I'm gay, and I'm happy.

Ignorance

My Sunday school teacher condemned sex. She said it was dirty until marriage. That didn't make sense.

Most of what we were told regarding sex did not make sense—especially when we were children:

- Sex is sinful, so save it for the one you love.
- If you masturbate, you will go blind.
- Men give women babies.
- If a boy plays with dolls, he could easily become homosexual.

Not one of these statements makes sense, but their intention was to make young people fear sex. Sex was seen as the enemy. Sex was a force for evil that needed to be avoided at all cost.

It had the opposite effect for most of us: Sex became the fascination.

I seek to heal my unhealthy childhood messages.

Shame

My parents had sex with the lights off. That tells you something.

The preceding statement tells us that shame is involved in many people's understanding of sexuality.

Why is this so? We know that some religions have at different times in history indicated that spirituality is *outside* the body—that the body is essentially sinful and dirty, harboring our animal instincts. Our sexual parts are usually *covered*, rarely seen, and shrouded in mystery. Churches have only recently explored the human pleasure associated with sex rather than preaching that sex's only purpose is procreation.

We begin to see from this background that what was hidden or forbidden becomes strangely attractive. And we know from the literature concerning sex addiction that it begins and grows in the hidden areas of a person's life.

We must respectfully shine the light on our sexual behavior.

*I am beginning to bring my
sexuality into the light.*

Unhealthy Messages

*A priest told me that really good boys give up
sex forever—that it's a gift to Jesus.*

I've always felt that sex addiction is enmeshed with
unhealthy religious teachings—that it's an aspect of
religious abuse that has created much fear, shame, and
guilt around all things sexual. In this toxic arena, sexual
compulsivity has thrived—but always in secret.

People were asked to deny a part of themselves and
then to offer it to God. Few were able to do this, and so
a Jekyll and Hyde existence developed that progressively
led to sex addiction.

For many people the only way to survive abusive
teachings was to be dishonest, to lie to the religious
people representing God. Unfortunately, we are as sick as
our secrets.

*Today I embrace a spiritual life
based upon honesty.*

Abuse

*My sister introduced me to sex. She was four
years older than I. For years my sister and I
had secret sex.*

I've heard variations on this theme for years as I have
consulted treatment centers that seek to heal sex
addiction. We can only imagine the guilt and shame that
young people have experienced as they lived and
remembered their "secret sex."

Psychiatrists and therapists who have studied sex
addiction tell us that as long as past behaviors and inci-
dents remain hidden, it is impossible for healing to begin.

Most children explore the fascination of sex—often
with their siblings. Spirituality is the catalyst that can
enable people to find their strength, share their shame,
and not wallow in a victim's guilt.

*Today I understand that I was a child
and that I should not feel guilty.*

Hell

*I knew I was going to hell if I continued to
masturbate. I continued!*

I remember hearing a teacher at school say that people
do what they want to do. Few people do not enjoy
masturbation. Most people do it or create a variation on
the activity.

Spirituality embraces masturbation. Sex is part of the
human condition, and we should not feel any shame
because we find pleasure in masturbating. Historically,
religion has condemned it. Some ministers created "holy
fear" by suggesting that masturbation would take mas-
turbators into the gates of hell. Thank God this attitude
is in decline—but only recently. The shame associated
with masturbation still echoes in the corridors of most
religions.

We do what comes naturally, and that is a key ingredient toward sexual healing.

*I am pursuing educated
religious teachings.*

Intimacy

I'm in my fifties, and I'm just discovering what intimacy really means: I'm understanding respectful sex.

I had a friend state the preceding to me with tears in his eyes. For twenty years we had both gone to recovery meetings for alcoholism, but I didn't know he also was a sex addict. I appreciated his honesty.

He shared that for most of his life he had thought that sex was something that you "do" to a person or allow them to "do" to you and that you had not "had sex" unless you climaxed or had an orgasm. In his recovery for sex addiction, he was discovering the spiritual power of intimacy: doing things *with* another person. That need not involve more than holding or gently stroking a person— and an orgasm need not be involved.

My friend was creating a spiritual gentleness that allowed for sexual healing.

*Today I have a deeper understanding
of sex, and I respect it.*

31

A Gift

I believe the gift of sex comes from God.
Essentially, sex is spiritual.

I have taught for years that healthy sexual expression is spiritual.

Invariably, people who have suffered from sex addiction or sexual compulsivity have believed that they are sinful or dirty because their religious teachers told them that sex, other than in marriage, was sinful or dirty. Alternatively, sex was not talked about; nobody mentioned it. If it occurred in the house, it happened in silence and in the shadows.

All of this has helped to foster covert behavior around sex addiction. Today we must affirm clearly that sex is an expression of love. Sex enables physical intimacy, and healthy sexuality requires respect and is always respectful.

For the sex addict, the healing begins when you respect your own sexuality and are respectful of others.

Spirituality demands respect.

12 Step

Why do I need to go to a 12 Step program for my sex addiction? I go to church regularly.

You don't have to go to a 12 Step program. I've met people who are recovering from different types of addiction who do not go to 12 Step meetings. Alcoholics are recovering within their families, drug addicts have returned to their religious organizations with a different attitude, and healing has undeniably taken place. The saying "Different strokes for different folks" comes to mind.

However, most people who are recovering from addiction, including sex addiction, are recovering within 12 Step support groups around the country, indeed the world. It is the best bet in town!

At meetings, people get a chance to share their feelings with other addicts in a nonprofessional setting. No real financial cost is incurred. The program has a spiritual foundation rather than a religious affiliation—and it offers suggestions only.

God, I express my gratitude for the variety of help that is available to me.

Healing

*I used to think that my sex addiction affected
only me, but it culminated in my divorce.*

Alcoholics and addicts often think that their problem
affects only them, but therapists have shown that
addiction is a "family disease." This is also true about sex
addiction.

It is not just the sexual escapades that prove to be
unbearable—but also the lies, manipulation, and sustained covert behavior.

For this reason therapy for *all* addicts embraces spirituality: moving into a complete overhaul of destructive
behavior and negative thinking. We create a recovery
process that affirms positive thinking and creative behavior in *all* areas of our lives, and this must include relationships. We develop a spiritual program that affirms
honesty, straightforwardness, and a healthy lifestyle that
in turn allows for progressive healing.

*Today I know that my sex addiction has affected
all my significant relationships, and I seek a
comprehensive healing.*

Education

When I mention sex addiction, people laugh.
And I laugh with them. But it's not funny.

Sex is often discussed as a joke; not in every case, but more often than not, the embarrassment that we feel is covered by humor. Historically, sex has been private, excluded from polite conversations, hidden by covert behavior. Many reasons account for this, but religious morality has played a significant role.

I was raised to believe that sex was dirty and sinful outside of marriage. I remember my mother turning off the television when sex was portrayed on the screen. I never had a serious conversation with my parents about sex—except as a joke.

And I'm not alone. Most people have experienced a "guilty silence" pertaining to human sexuality. That is the root of the challenge in discussing and getting help for sexual compulsivity, so we must break the silence.

My spiritual journey
treats sex seriously.

Shame

I believe I love my wife. But when she discovered that I was looking at pornography on the Internet, I fell into silence. I'm so ashamed.

Sex addiction affects the family. In this case, the wife actually *saw* what her husband had been looking at on the Internet, and it inevitably created a shock, a trauma.

Maybe the husband does love his wife, but loving a person does not ensure that you will not hurt him or her. It is the human condition to hurt the people we love—none of us are perfect. That being the case, though, is no excuse for being unwilling to change the behavior that is creating the damage.

As a therapist, I would suggest that the wife and husband get into therapy. Indeed the whole family should do so if children are involved. I would also make it clear that it is okay for all family members to express and feel their hurt feelings because they are real.

The healing will be a process. It will take time.

I am willing to embrace the process of healing.

Self-Esteem

I'm gay, and I'm proud, but I'm not proud of my sexual compulsivity.

Sexual compulsivity is not exclusively related to the gay community, and so it is healthy for a person to feel a certain pride about their sexual preference. It is equally healthy that a person should be concerned or worried about developing a behavior concerning sexual compulsivity.

What can anyone do about sexually compulsive behaviors? I think it is important to see a therapist who specializes in the area of sex addiction. The conversation should begin with what the sexual compulsivity looks like, how it manifests itself.

Although this is easier said than done, no one should feel too guilty or ashamed. Many people become compulsive about a variety of things, and sexual compulsivity is a growing problem in our society, indeed the world.

*My spiritual journey
involves therapy.*

Compassion

I was sexually abused when I was seven.
Something froze inside me. Now I'm attracted
to little girls who are about seven.

It has often been said that the abused can easily grow up to become an abuser. I distinctly remember the man who shared this while speaking about his self-loathing with tears in his eyes. He hated who he had become. He hated his sexual nature!

It was Dr. Walther Lechler, who lives in Germany, who shared with me the concept that a trauma could "freeze" an individual, keeping him or her emotionally stunted *at the age of the abuse*. The man I have quoted here remained seven years old emotionally.

The man quoted here didn't grow up. It might take years of therapy to heal his childhood abuse and assist him in moving away from his attraction to little girls. The spiritual components of love, compassion, and hope would be essential in his healing.

I believe in the therapeutic process
that can provide healing.

Ignorance

My minister said sex was a problem in the Garden of Eden. It's still a problem.

The truth is that we do not know exactly what the problem was concerning Adam and Eve in the Garden of Eden. The biblical text certainly seems to reveal pride, arrogance, disobedience—but not sex. Yet according to the popular understanding, sex was the offense that led God to exile the unhappy couple from the Garden of Eden. Maybe the fact that Adam and Eve were naked created the confusion!

So sex was seen, and is still seen by many, to be the unforgivable offense that some call *original sin*. Ignorance has created shame.

People who have issues concerning sex often hide in the shadows because, instead of seeing themselves as sick, they see themselves as bad or sinful.

Education plays a major role in the healing of sex addiction.

*I'm slowly healing my
sexual shame.*

Subtle

Sex is subtly being pushed on regular television shows.

It is probably an exaggeration to say that sex is every-where, but it certainly seems to be playing a more significant role in regular television shows. Sex, rather than the story line, is used to sell shows, and it becomes more important than it really is.

Sex also helps to sell advertising, and that creates a society that often appears obsessed with sex. It certainly feeds the sex addict and his or her compulsive behavior. It is not unusual for me to hear clients share that they fantasize and masturbate while watching television shows that display sex.

Boundaries are essential in treating sex addiction, and some therapists regulate what can be watched on television. *Baywatch*, for example, was ruled out by almost all therapists!

My sex addiction recovery involves having healthy boundaries concerning my use of television.

True Cost

I'm only twenty-four years old, and I'm spending at least $2,000 per month for sex videos and prostitutes!

The 12 Step program says that addiction creates feelings of powerlessness and unmanageability in life, and those often have a direct effect on the checkbook.

Sex addicts spend an incredible amount of money on prostitution and explicit material, often hiding their expenses from family, friends, and loved ones. The slippery slope to despair has begun and looks like this:

- Credit card debt
- Lies to family, friends, and lovers
- Feelings of guilt and shame
- Suicidal thoughts
- Increasing Internet pornography addiction
- Irresponsible manipulation of family expenses

The recovery stressing the need for personal honesty and transparency has helped other addicts and awaits all in need.

Economic security is an aspect of my spiritual journey.

Intimacy

I thought for years that intimacy was having sex.

Most people would think "Was the relationship sexual?" when they hear the question "Were you intimate with this person?" But intimacy expressed in this way provides a very narrow definition of what the word *intimate* actually means. Sex and intimacy are not the same.

A powerful aspect of therapy often includes psychodrama, and I've experienced therapists doing some powerful work with sex addicts on how to develop loving and intimate relationships that would not be considered sexual.

- An intimate, yet nonsexual, hug
- A gentle nonsexual stroking of a person's back or shoulders to reveal caring
- Gentle words spoken within the context of a safe and loving affection

Intimacy can be romantic and yet nonsexual.

Great Spirit, I seek to be gentle
in my relationships.

Healing

*I can't resist going to sex sites on the Internet.
Then I enter the chat rooms. Afterward I feel so
disgusted with myself.*

Why does this person feel such self-disgust? Therapists will tell you that the guilt and shame come from the explicit nature of what is discussed in these chat rooms.

As I've stressed throughout this book, spiritually we want to celebrate the precious gift of sexuality, but sex addiction takes you to that dark place where your personal morals and integrity are degraded by your addiction. Crude talk, explicit sexual behavior discussed with strangers, dishonesty—all run rampant to maintain the sick fantasy.

As a sex addict shared with me in her early months of recovery, "My sex addiction took me into the sewer. I felt dirty after each sex binge."

*My recovery from sex addiction
makes me feel clean.*

Hope

I lost a job because I was sexually inappropriate at work. I'm still sexually inappropriate in my new job. And I'm afraid.

It is true that some people who are sexually inappropriate do not have a sex addiction. That can be likened to the way that not all people who get a D.U.I. are alcoholics. But many sex addicts obviously take their compulsivity to work with them, and their powerlessness and unmanageability create inappropriate behavior.

Of course sex addicts are afraid, but they must connect responsibility to their fear. Sex addiction is treatable. People are recovering in support programs. Many are able to forgive themselves for past behaviors and are living a spiritual program. Hope is alive.

I am responsible for my behaviors.

Recovery

I went to my first sex addiction meeting and was able to identify with many of the people sharing. Now I know I'm not alone.

It is hard to believe that some compulsive eaters believe that they are the only people in the world who eat compulsively. Some addicts, men and women, think that they are alone with their particular problem. This is certainly true when it comes to people engaged in sexually compulsive behavior. They think their experience—the shame of being a compulsive masturbator, the guilt and secrecy involved in watching pornography on a computer, the financial worry created by regular visits to sex clubs and prostitutes—is unique, but they are not alone.

Support groups for people suffering from sex addiction are among the fastest-growing 12 Step programs in the country, and people are getting help when they decide to come out from the shadows.

Today I know that I am not alone.

Triggers

*I am hooked on phone sex. Then I call out for a
prostitute. But the phone sex is my "trigger."*

I often see late-night television advertisements for
phone sex: Attractive young women, usually dressed
in an alluring negligee or bathing suit, suggest that you
phone them because they will meet your every need!

Phone sex is identified in the preceding quotation as
the trigger that leads to prostitutes. The following are
some triggers I have heard from patients receiving treatment for sex addiction:

- Certain clothes that stimulate a fantasy
- A type of cologne
- Consumption of alcohol
- Drug use
- Viewing of a porno movie

Then the phone sex follows.

The key to recovery is breaking down the denial and
seeking help.

***I must replace my addictive rituals
with rituals of healing.***

Love

Love is everything.

I believe that love is everything. I hold the opinion that spirituality is the foundation for living "the good life" and that this must involve a concept of love. Many definitions and explanations apply to love; some include sex.

For many years, especially in religious circles, sex has been played down in general discussions of love, but maybe that must change. Sex—and, more important, sexuality—is an important expression of our physical needs and desires, which are not unimportant. From sexual intercourse to a passionate embrace, our sexuality is involved—and it is good . . . noble . . . divine.

Can our sexuality become diseased and dysfunctional? Absolutely. But the human attributes of sexuality are a most precious gift.

Thank you for the sexual
aspect of my love.

Responsibility

Sex is not dirty or immoral; however, I must act responsibly and respect God's gift.

At different times I write in this book that sex is not dirty, that it is a gift from God, an aspect of love. Having said this, I also must state clearly that we always must act responsibly when we consider sexual expression.

Indeed, for many people sex has become a curse, a tragic personal defect that is destroying them, their families, and their significant relationships. Sex has become a core addiction that leads a growing number of addicts back to abusing drugs and alcohol. In other cases, their sex addiction leads to drugs or other unhealthy behaviors. All this happens in tandem with what we know about sexually transmitted diseases, including AIDS.

Sex is a gift that demands respect.

Today I respect my sexuality, and
I respect the sexuality of others.

Insanity

*I had sex with a stranger at my wedding party.
I'm disgusted with myself.*

It is healthy to feel disgusted with yourself for having sex on your wedding day; however, more is required than feeling disgusted. What are you going to do about it?

Aspects of sex addiction are epidemic in our society because few people seek treatment and recovery. Recovery is happening for alcoholics and drug addicts because, thanks to people like Betty Ford and actor Anthony Hopkins, more and more people are talking about what it was like to live with their addictions. We hope more people will seek therapy and recovery for their sex addiction.

Being disgusted is fine for a week or more, but eventually the sex addict must get off the pity pot and move into healing. The recovery and shame will only be removed when people begin to talk and share openly about what it was like to live with their sex addiction.

*In an atmosphere of safety, I will
share my feelings of shame.*

Criminality

I inappropriately touched a young boy in the swimming pool. Nobody saw me. I am so ashamed.

These words were shared with me by a married man who was in treatment for his addictive sexual behavior. I remember him saying that sometimes the compulsive feelings within him were so strong that he could not resist acting out. How close he came to being arrested! And what damage he had caused to the young boy!

Treatment seeks to show that the message in his head that says he cannot resist certain feelings is untrue. He needs a new message that talks about creating healthy boundaries. He must begin talking about his pedophilic feelings and receive therapy for the secret behavior that has been cloaked behind being a married man. His wife and family would need, eventually, to be involved. That's major work. No doubt, painful secrets will be revealed. It's all the price of his move toward healing.

Although painful,
I will reveal my secrets.

Sex Advertising

I spend twenty minutes every day cleaning the sexual advertising that is sent to me by unsolicited e-mail.

These comments were made to me recently by my office manager. I took a look and was amazed at what was being advertised:

- Viagra at discount prices
- A pill to enlarge a penis
- A vagina cream that helps to create unlimited orgasms, without a partner
- Sex toys for the adventurous
- Barely legal sex videotapes

The emphasis upon sex in our society is increasing at an incredible rate, and this surely plays a role in the rise of sex addiction. Will it ever go away? No. We must develop healthy boundaries so that we remain sexually healthy.

Healthy boundaries are part of my living the spiritual life.

Relapse

Sex is my real focus, and I use alcohol and drugs to act out sexually.

A close friend shared this statement with me recently after having had numerous treatments for alcohol and drug abuse—and as many relapses. During his many months of treatment, he never discussed his sex addiction issues. He said he felt too guilty. Too much shame. Some things were too personal to discuss, even with a therapist!

These sentiments are true for many people who have received drug and alcohol treatment or who are presently undergoing treatment and are experiencing the shame that creates secrecy.

I'm pleased he has now recognized the need to be honest about his sexual compulsivity, and I'm equally pleased to be able to write about it. Others may be prompted to begin the process of sharing their sexual compulsivity as it relates to their alcohol and drug use.

*Confronting my secrets is the key
to my spiritual awakening.*

Living On the Edge

I had unprotected sex in a parking garage with a stranger. I still don't know his name!

The second step from the 12 Step program says it clearly:

> Came to believe that a Power greater than ourselves could restore us to sanity.

Am I suggesting that the sex addict is insane? In a poetic sense, yes. To have unprotected sex in a parking garage with a stranger, knowing what we know about sexually transmitted diseases and AIDS—yes, that's crazy. I also believe that sexual compulsivity is a treatable sickness, as are alcoholism and gambling addiction.

The stories I've heard in alcoholism support programs often shock and amaze me. It is no different with sex addiction, and a similar process of treatment is required for daily recovery.

I know my sex addiction
is treatable.

Nobody's Perfect

I went to a therapist for my compulsive sexual behavior, and my therapist behaved inappropriately: he suggested I go on a date with him.

For years I've known people who were alcohol and drug abuse counselors who were *active* addicts; they hoped to get help and recovery by simply working around it. Few lasted; most went into treatment for their own issues.

Psychiatrists, psychologists, therapists, and clergy are not perfect; knowledge does not make a person healthy. This is certainly true for the professionals who work with sex addicts.

Boundaries, working a personal recovery program, and seeking to live the spiritual life would seem essential for those of us who work with addicts, and it is undeniably true that sharing our personal woundedness creates healing.

However, it is unacceptable to prey on the addict seeking help, and professionals who do so must be reported.

I am a wounded healer, not a
healer who wounds!

Religious Abuse

The preacher said he would show me what God's love was like, but it was our secret.

The recent cases involving sexual abuse by clergy have created a scandal that has shocked many. Some people have stopped going to their church, mosque, synagogue, or temple. Religious abuse that involves sex has probably been around forever, but it is only recently that people have discovered the courage to speak out and report it.

This aspect of religious abuse, alongside the sexual abuse, is particularly appalling because it draws into the abuse our concept of and relationship with God. As one lady shared with me, "It was as if God were raping me!"

It is my belief that sex addiction and sexual compulsivity are meshed with religious abuse. Indeed, the shame that leads to secrecy is often connected with a person's understanding of sin.

Spiritually, I understand that religious abuse hurts my appreciation of God.

Powerlessness

I had admitted I was powerless over alcohol and drugs. When I discovered the sex site on the Internet, I felt powerless all over again.

It is sometimes said that addicts suffer from cross-addiction: When they have stopped doing a particular behavior, they develop another obsession; when a person stops smoking, he or she can easily gravitate to compulsive eating.

A therapist friend of mine calls it "filling the hole." When we have given up experiencing a particular "high," we look for something that will provide another escape, another "trip."

I personally feel that many addicts have a sexual compulsivity and that the sex addiction comes to the forefront when they stop using their substance of choice. Then the feeling of powerlessness returns.

Fortunately, 12 Step groups provide support that has proved helpful for other addicts and alcoholics.

*I seek recovery for my sex addiction
in a spiritual support group.*

Guilt

*I began masturbating with my brother when
I was nine or ten. I'm thirty years old now,
and I still feel guilty.*

In discussing the subject of masturbation, I learned that
many people feel guilty. Much of the guilt follows religious instruction that condemned masturbation as a sin,
implying that the "spilling of the seed" was tantamount
to a waste of life.

Interestingly, this logic hardly applies to female
masturbation!

People usually discover sex and masturbation, as the
preceding statement confirms, within the family or with
friends. People play "Doctor and Patient" and discover
more about their bodies. At about the same time, religion
and moral guilt work their way into our thinking, reprimanding us with "Bad boy!" and worse for masturbating.

Time and education will prove to be the essential healers, although we must always respect, even if we do not
agree with, the morally binding customs of all religious
traditions.

Today I appreciate every aspect of my body.

Healthy Love

I don't think I ever understood the difference between love and sex.

For years I believed that showing love involved some aspect of sexual behavior: a kiss, fondle, or intimate grope. Love involved "getting off" with somebody.

On reflection, this is a slight exaggeration because I appreciated the love of my family and friends, and sex was not involved. However, outside of such specific areas, sex was love and love involved sex.

Today I am able to love without having to be sexual. I can appreciate a person's looks, personality, and behavior without needing to grope or go to bed together. I'm able to create spiritual boundaries in my life, and although my mind might occasionally wander into sexual fantasies, mostly I'm loving them for who they are. That feels good. It feels healthy.

Today I can love without feeling shame.

Self-Disgust

When the sex urge comes upon me, I don't like who I am.

When I was first facing my alcoholic behavior, I remember a therapist telling me the story of Dr. Jekyll and Mr. Hyde. Like many people, I had read the book as a child and had seen the movies, but I had never contemplated the story in the context of alcoholism. When I revisited the story, I could identify with the fear and shame that Dr. Jekyll experienced when he contemplated his behavior as Mr. Hyde.

He did not like who he had become.

The sex addict is no different, but it is important to remember that we are more than the behavior that causes us shame. I believe that we can all reflect a divine goodness. If we choose—and it will certainly require some effort on our part—we can heal negative thinking and destructive behaviors.

I choose to be a positive
and creative person.

Pornography

I spend hours most nights looking at pornography on the Internet.

Can you imagine the amount of time and money that is wasted by sex addicts viewing content on the Internet? No wonder pornography is a billion-dollar business.

But this is looking at pornography and the Internet in broad-brush terms. What about the havoc such behavior causes the individual, the family, or friendships? When we talk in general terms, we forget individuals' tears, shame, fear, despair, and pain.

Actually, the pain is good because it is what will spur the intervention that leads—hopefully—to recovery. As 12 Step people say, "No gain without pain."

The tragedy is the denial and covert behavior that keep the sexual compulsivity alive and secret.

*Great Spirit, thank you for the pain
that led me into recovery.*

Manipulation

I was sexually abused by my uncle at the age of ten, but I should not use this tragedy to avoid taking responsibility for my sex addiction.

Many therapists see a connection between a young person's sexual abuse and the development of sex addiction in later life. However, it must be clearly stated that not all sex addicts or sexually compulsive people were abused as children. Many people develop a sex addiction as adults, or even as children, without being sexually abused.

Spiritually, the issue is to take responsibility for what we are doing in our lives. Addiction, in all its guises, is healed by a change in behavior. What we do affects who we eventually become.

I take responsibility for what happens in my life.

God's Gift

Sex is a gift from God.

When we speak about sex addiction or sexual compulsivity issues, especially pornography, child abuse, and a variety of fetishes, it is so easy to forget that sex—human sexuality—is a precious gift from God. Even if you are agnostic or atheist, it is important to recognize that love and intimacy are achieved through the gift of human sexuality.

How do we hold onto the idea of sex as a gift? Well, maybe we must put sex within the perspective of what it is to be human. When we say that human beings are imperfect, it means that we all face certain challenges, and we all abuse or misuse aspects of life. Some people eat, drink alcohol, or work too much, and yet they are able to address the problem and experience recovery. In a similar way, we can heal our damaged sexuality and come to appreciate the gift.

God, thank you for the gift of sex.

March

Inquiry

What is a sex addict?

This is a complicated question that is not easily answered within a short reading. The 12 Step program, which has proven to be most helpful to recovering alcoholics, suggests that addiction is present when the associated behaviors and feelings of powerlessness have become unmanageable.

For the sex addict, this might be seen in the following:

- Arguments with significant others that are caused by unhealthy sexual behavior
- Feelings of despair and self-loathing related to sexual activities
- Legal issues resulting from sexual activities
- Secretive behavior around sex
- Sexual behavior that is accompanied by lies and denial
- Constantly thinking about sex

The spiritual solution comes in acknowledging these real concerns and having the willingness to ask for help.

*I am a sex addict desirous of
treatment and recovery.*

Crime

I recently shared with a therapist that I raped my girlfriend and that it wasn't the first time. She clearly said "No," but I couldn't control my sexual urges. I know I need help.

Most rapes are not reported, and date-rape is more common than most people imagine. Tragically, women sometimes stay with their rapists and don't report the rape!

Sexual crimes create such twisted shame that the victim often feels guilty and the perpetrator hopes that this shame will maintain the secrecy.

Sex addicts occasionally commit sexual crimes. For this reason, the spiritual theme for sexual healing is to seek help and have the willingness to undergo therapy, to talk honestly about what is actually happening, and to create a program for healing.

We celebrate the power of therapy and recovery in these pages.

Because I have a healthy fear of where my sex addiction could lead, I seek therapy.

Dysfunction

*I slept with my mother until I was twelve.
I remember my mother and I masturbated each
other. Today I'm a compulsive masturbator, and I
often think about those times with my mother.
What should I do?*

So often we find that what happened in the family
stays in the family. It is beneficial to connect what
happened with a parent to one's current compulsive
sexual behavior. The spiritual intent is to want to do
something about it, to want healing.

When we are introduced to a behavior that brings
euphoria—an intense sense of pleasure at an early age—
it can easily develop into an addiction, such as compulsive masturbation.

Getting into therapy for any childhood abuse is essential,
coupled with attending a support group that addresses sex
addiction. Change occurs when we get connected with a
recovery process that brings hope and healing.

*Spiritually, I'm ready to discuss my sexual abuse
and connect it with my sexual behavior.*

Sexsomnia

My girlfriend falls asleep for a few hours and then occasionally starts masturbating.

It is the opinion of many psychiatrists that our subconscious plays a powerful role in our lives and that we may not always be aware of why we do what we do. This includes what happens during sleep. Having sex while asleep—touching our partners, making definite and sustained sexual advances, and such—could indicate serious sexual issues that might require therapeutic healing, and the behavior, known clinically as *sexsomnia*, could cause additional problems—for example, physical abuse or rape. It is not unusual for the partner of the person suffering from sexsomnia to seek a separation or divorce.

We are as sick as our secrets. Not talking about sexsomnia is a serious mistake. Spiritually, it is important to remember that knowledge about how and why we behave in a certain way is the key to healing and lasting change. Therapy is becoming an important adjunct to spiritual transformation and wellness.

I am not afraid to discuss my sexual behavior with people I trust.

Denial

*I'm a therapist who treated people for sex
addiction, but I didn't get help for my own
sex addiction until I was arrested in a sting
operation that included a fifteen-year-old girl.*

Clergy are not saints. Neither are therapists. We all
have our demons to face.

Some professionals seek to help people who have issues
similar to their own, but that is dangerous and unprofessional if they have not first faced their own dysfunction and sought help, which will often include therapy.

Recovery cannot occur by osmosis. Helping addicts
is no substitute for getting help for oneself, especially for
similar issues. The preceding story is tragic, but perhaps
it will be read by someone who is in a similar situation
and will get help before a disaster occurs.

A powerful spiritual message is that there are right
words that come to us at the right time. Are you listening?

*Spiritually, I understand the powerful
words, "Physician, heal thyself."*

Progression

My sexual compulsivity has progressed over the years. I'm now into people slapping and hurting me: The pain excites me.

Most of us think that sadomasochistic sex is practiced by only a few people, but in my ongoing research about sex addiction and sexual compulsivity I've come to realize that this behavior is a significant part of many people's lives.

I am helped in understanding the move toward sadomasochism in terms of the *progressive theory*. Using drugs as an example, a person might start with alcohol and marijuana and then eventually progress to using heroin. True, some may start their drug use with heroin, but for most addicts it is progressive.

The sex addict may be involved similarly in a progression: girlie magazines, masturbation, bisexual games—moving toward experiences of sadomasochism.

An aspect of spiritual healing will involve a respect of ourselves and others, beginning with a realistic fear of unheeded consequences.

Today I respect my body enough never to hurt it.

Letting Go

Lent for me, even though I don't go to church anymore, is a time of personal sacrifice. This Lent I embrace therapy, and I'm learning to let go of my compulsive behavior.

L ent is always a special time for me, beginning with the ritual on Ash Wednesday that reminds me, poetically, that I came from the earth and I will one day return to the earth: dust to dust, ashes to ashes. Lent helps keep me humble.

During past Lents I have given up cigarettes, alcohol, and desserts, and these little sacrifices remind me that I have the power to create discipline in my life, that I am powerful over my choices.

The recovery word *surrender* seems appropriate for the Lenten season—maybe some of us must *let go* of *what we want to do* and begin moving toward *what we must do.* Perhaps we should reevaluate whether we need more therapy, treatment, recovery groups, or a sponsor, all of which have historically kept people healthy.

I enjoy making healthy choices in my life.

Sharing

I'm so happy that we have so many support meetings in the city where I live. I share and listen. It's been four years since I've acted out sexually.

It is important to know that people are recovering from sex addiction. Often we hear only about the people who are in despair or facing tragic consequences—but many people are healing one day at a time.

12 Step meetings for sex addiction are springing up all over because of the growing need. More and more treatment centers are cognizant of the symptoms of sexual compulsivity that create relapse for alcoholics and other addicts.

Spirituality is about reality: seeing things for what they are rather than living in denial. Only recently has sex addiction been brought to the attention of the general public and the greater addiction community, thanks in part to the pioneer work of Dr. Patrick Carnes. And yes, people are healing and recovering one day at a time.

I celebrate the recovery that is happening for many sex addicts.

Exhibitionism

I'm a young man, and I like to show my penis to other men in a public restroom. I sometimes visit ten restrooms in a day.

*E*xhibitionism: an aspect of sex addiction. *Exhibitionist:* someone who flashes others in public to get attention, someone who runs naked down a street or across a football field, as well as the young man who focuses his pride and self-esteem solely on his penis.

Psychiatrists have often discovered, however, that at their core exhibitionists have a low opinion of themselves; their shocking behavior conceals a perverse self-loathing. Their neediness reveals a belief that they are essentially "less than" others. Exhibitionism is an aspect of sex addiction that reveals a person who is spiritually broken.

Recovery teaches us that what is broken can be fixed. Healing is available for those who are willing to seek help. The focus of therapy for the exhibitionist is to develop self-esteem and self-love.

I show respect for others by developing personal boundaries and a healthy love of who I am.

Embarrassment

I feel guilty because I don't respect my parents. I'm a teenager, and I'm embarrassed at how my parents behave when my friends are over. Their sex talk is disturbing.

Studies in alcoholism teach us that alcoholics seek out other alcoholics with whom to drink, drug addicts find other drug addicts with whom to use drugs, and sex addicts will often seek out other sex addicts to form relationships.

Those of us who work in the field of addiction must educate the general public about sexual compulsivity issues, and this must include going into schools and colleges. Children and teenagers must be informed that help is available if their parents are sexually inappropriate, as well as where they can go to get help.

When we seek a spiritual solution to dysfunctional relationships, it is important that we provide helpful interventions that lead to healing and recovery. We want to keep a family together whenever possible, and a key ingredient for this connection is respect.

My behavior affects those I love.

An Awakening

*I had a powerful spiritual awakening in
treatment for my sex addiction. I realized that
I was not a bad person, that I have a sickness!*

It is true that many people have a moment of awareness
in their recovery process that is often called a *spiritual
awakening*.

An important breakthrough, especially for sex addiction, occurs when the person recognizes that he or she is
not bad or sinful and has a sickness.

Sex addiction probably has more toxic shame attached
to it than any other addiction does. Indeed, we know
that sexuality tends to live in the shadows, often hidden
behind a rigid morality, even for people who do not have
a sex addiction.

It is therefore incredibly important, indeed it is a spiritual awakening, for the sex addict to understand that he or
she has a sickness, a disease, and is not alone. This often
prompts the person to seek help from a professional, and
then the ensuing therapy becomes an exciting adventure.

*Great Spirit, I cooperate with you
in my healing process.*

The Process

I heard a psychiatrist suggest that letting go was essential in the healing of sexual compulsivity. How do I let go of a sex addiction?

Everyone has had to let go of something or someone at some point in their lives, but in the case of sex addiction, this process can only be achieved if we go gently. To rush would create a disaster.

A letting-go process that I have found helpful is this:

- I take time to think seriously about what I wish to let go of; often I will write down behaviors and thoughts as they come to mind.
- It is important to find someone with whom to share my behaviors and thoughts, someone I trust, who will nurture me toward recovery.
- Then I must do it, even though procrastination is a character defect I possess, especially when it comes to my personal issues.

When we follow these simple steps, we begin the journey into spiritual healing.

Today I embrace the process of letting go.

Obsession

I love having sex. I think about it all the time.
No girlfriend will stay with me because I'm too
demanding. Recently I've been using prostitutes.

I think it is important to recognize that women suffer from sex addiction as much as men and are often tormented by the added judgment of being a bad mother, a disrespectful wife, a whore.

In our sexualized society, sex addiction is growing astronomically. Clearly the consequences are disastrous if a person does not get help. This help involves moving into a spiritual program:

• Having a God of love and not judgment
• Understanding that sex addiction is not bad or sinful but rather a treatable illness
• Attending spiritual support groups

Whatever the sexual challenge might be, help is available.

Knowing that I am not alone
helps heal the shame.

Family Sickness

I'm worried about my son. I divorced his father
because he was a sex addict. Now my son seems
obsessed with pornography.

I remember hearing a therapist share that the word *discipline* is linked to the spiritual word *disciple*, inferring that if we want to follow "the high road" we must enforce healthy boundaries.

Some actions are not okay. Children should not be allowed to do what they want just because they want to do it. It is okay to say "No."

It is certainly possible that the wife of a sex addict will develop her own low self-esteem and neediness. We know that it is a healthy thing to divorce a sexually addictive husband who will not get treatment; however, a mother must make another healthy choice by getting help for her children.

The spiritual solution for families involves more than prayer—it requires therapy.

I pray, but I also move my feet
in the direction of healing.

Geographicals

I've been to Thailand six times this year. And all I do is pay for sex. I live to go to Thailand.

I wonder how this person feels. What must it be like to always want to be elsewhere—and all for sex?

We know that many sex addicts go on advertised "sex holidays," during which they can binge on sex, if they can afford it, morning, noon, and night. Child sex is often included.

Governments are becoming aware of the sex-slave business, and more and more people are caught and arrested for it. But are they merely criminals? My belief is that many are sex addicts who are sorely in need of help and treatment.

The spiritual solution is not to deny any compulsivity that might be involved in such "sex holidays" but to engage in a healthier long-term solution that addresses the treatable addiction and compulsivity that clearly destroy families and society.

Hopefully, sex addicts will find help and healing before they find themselves in prison!

Today I seek to treat all people with respect.

Spirituality

My therapist says I must find a spiritual solution for my sex addiction.

Spirituality is seen by many therapists as essential in the healing of addiction, and this obviously includes sex addiction that is permeated with guilt and toxic shame.

But what is the spiritual model? Different people have a variety of suggestions, but this is what it involves for me:

- A clear distinction between the role of religion and the more inclusive definition of spirituality
- A holistic healing of the body, mind, and emotions
- Positive and creative actions
- A linkage with the "spiritual awakening" promised in 12 Step programs
- Spirituality is my life

I embrace a spirituality
that is based on respect for other
people's beliefs and culture.

Holidays

Friends of mine got drunk on St. Patrick's Day.
While they were drinking, I searched for sex.
Holidays fuel my sex addiction.

Women have shared similar stories. During holidays they would find places to hang out so that they could get picked up. They had little interest in alcohol or drugs, which they used only to find a sex partner. A feeling of dysthymia or depression always followed; occasionally, it would lead to thoughts or attempts of suicide.

We know that isolation is an enemy of recovery for the addict, and we certainly see this behavior described here. The solution is to get the sex addict involved in the healing process, talking with other sex addicts, and feeling the nurturing support that comes with attending meetings regularly.

I celebrate that my sexual compulsivity and
depression are treatable.

Sexual Violence

I've always been a violent person. In recent years I've noticed that I get sexually stimulated when I fight with my wife. Seeing the fear on her face excites me sexually.

Sadism is not relegated solely to horror movies. It is the all-too-real euphoria that some people experience from inflicting pain on others or watching others suffer.

Many reasons or theories address why sadistic behavior begins. Whatever the cause, the sadist most likely to receive help is the one who feels guilty or ashamed after experiencing the euphoria created by an act of violence. Without remorse, the chances of receiving help are slim.

The preceding quotation comes from someone in recovery. He attends meetings regularly and is seeing a therapist. He is looking at the messages he received while growing up in a violent family and is replacing them with gentle affirmations. And he's not impatient for recovery.

I'm slowly talking about my most shameful sexual acts. I'm willing to go to any lengths for recovery.

The Hunt

*My girlfriends and I play a game: hunting for
sex. I've met other lesbians who do it, but I'm
always ashamed the next morning.*

When we enter the world of sex addiction or hear
the expressed behaviors of sexual compulsivity, we
will meet the games that people play. Perhaps another
word for *games* might be *rituals*. Such behaviors lead to
what is called "the hunt."

I believe that we live in an overly sexualized society,
and this involves not only men seeking women or men
seeking men but also women seeking other women. The
focus is on getting sex, with no appreciation of what a
real relationship might look like, and with even less
appreciation for the people involved.

A spiritual understanding of sex must be appreciated
and valued within the context of love and affection.
Recovery, at all times, presents us with the concept of
respect of self, others, and God.

*My personal healing requires
a willingness to heal my behaviors.*

Patience

I'm happy I have support groups for my sex addiction, but I'm still sexually compulsive. I've had sex occasionally with people who attend the support meetings.

I remember my sponsor saying to me that, as an alcoholic, I must choose my meetings carefully. This is also true for sex addicts. If you find that some of the people at meetings, either because of what they are saying or doing, are creating triggers for you, then leave. Talk to your sponsor. Perhaps you should return to therapy or go to therapy for the first time. Certainly, you can find different meetings to attend.

Crazy people, even in recovery, will create crazy outcomes, so remember we have the choice of who we talk with, go for coffee with, and get involved with at meetings.

Love and respect for oneself, as a sex addict, are often considered the key to future healthy relationships.

I choose my recovery meetings
and friendships carefully.

Isolation

My sex addiction has really isolated me from other people. I just sit in my room watching porno and reading "girlie" magazines.

Sometimes we must ask ourselves, "What is the quality of my life? Am I living life or merely existing?"

Isolation is common among sex addicts, an issue that all addicts eventually face. It is a slow and progressive withdrawal from life.

However, it is rare for isolation alone to be the reason that the sex addict seeks help. Usually other matters—divorce, legal issues, scandal, suicidal ideation—push sex addicts in the direction of professional help. Addicts seek help when they experience powerlessness and unmanageability.

Recovery will be experienced when the addict makes the decision to change the behaviors that are creating isolation and unhappiness. The sex addict emerges slowly from shame to discover healthy relationships and intimacy.

Today I confront my feelings of isolation
by going to support meetings.

Kindness

I hurt people when I was into my sex addiction.
Today I seek to be kind on a daily basis.

Addiction hurts the addict and family and friends. Addiction sometimes kills people other than the addict.

What our addiction was like is a central theme of any 12 Step program. We must see what the sickness looks like and what it did to the people we love. Recovery depends on breaking down the walls of selfishness and denial.

The opposite constitutes our spiritual program: The dishonest seek to be honest, the cruel work at being kind, the selfish seek to serve, and the arrogant work at being humble.

Knowing what I used to be like is the key
to the changes I am making in my life.

Change

My husband and I constantly argue about the way he leers at young women. He says he can't help it. What should I do?

Spirituality involves taking responsibility for one's own actions and behaviors. Most of the time, when a person says he cannot help it, it is usually an excuse. What he means is that he doesn't want to do anything about it, doesn't want to take responsibility for what he is doing, doesn't want to change.

It has been said that we teach people how to treat us. If no consequences are involved, a person rarely changes. Confrontation is often the first step toward healing, change, and recovery.

A powerful statement might be, "If you continue what you are doing and do not get help, then I will leave you. Because I love you, I'm willing to go with you to get help. But I must state my position clearly: Things must change."

The journey into recovery and healing involves painful consequences.

Voyeurism

I've not had sex for years. I don't masturbate, but I'm still obsessed with anything sexual. I like to watch people having sex. I've paid money to watch people. Am I a sex addict?

Sex addiction is not only about performance. It is the constant thinking and obsessing about sex that indicate the powerlessness and unmanageability.

When the person asks, "Am I a sex addict?" we know that the person is feeling extremely uncomfortable in areas that pertain to sexuality. For example, the individual is feeling guilty and ashamed for having to pay to watch people have sex, for engaging in voyeurism. But the question is answered when we hear, "I'm still obsessed with anything sexual." It is the obsession that reveals addiction, a complete lack of balance.

The sex addict knows when something is wrong and yet still pretends to be ignorant. A word that springs to mind is *denial*: not wanting to know what we know! The spiritual journey will inevitably lead to confronting denial in order to embrace reality.

I will confront my denial and seek help.

Masturbation

I secretly caught my father masturbating to pornography on the Internet. Today I hate to be around him, but I've not told my mother.

We all know that alcoholism affects the family. It causes major problems in any relationship. Sex addiction is no different.

Children rarely expect to see defects of character or imperfection in their parents. Inappropriate sexual behavior, if seen or discovered, can create a major trauma.

Unfortunately, with sex addiction, indeed with most aspects of sexuality, inappropriate sexual behavior is rarely discussed, tends to be covert, and is enveloped in silence. Parents rarely talk about sex with their children; children keep sexual secrets from their parents. Dysfunction, unhealthy behaviors, anger, and shame increase in this situation.

Healing is discovered in breaking the silence, in discussing what is difficult, in bringing the secrets to the light.

Spiritually, I am coming to understand that secrecy is dishonesty.

Addiction

Today I'm in prison for various sexual assaults that I committed as a younger man. I'm still seeking sex in prison. Is this what people call a "sex addiction"?

He'd been in prison for ten years, had a poor education, and had never, until recently, heard about sex addiction. But he genuinely wanted to know if he had "it."

I reminded him that the alcoholics in the group had defined their alcoholism based on their lives being powerless and unmanageable concerning alcohol: Step One of Alcoholics Anonymous.

Had his life been powerless and unmanageable around sex? Obviously—he was in prison!

He considered all the sex crimes against women he'd committed, including some for which he was put on trial. Sex had always consumed him, and he was now having unprotected sex with men.

After a short consideration, he said clearly, "I'm a sex addict." That was a spiritual awakening.

Only when I face the truth do I recognize my sex addiction.

Understanding

Can you be a sex addict if you don't have sex?

Actually, you can. There are sex addicts who do not actually *have* sex, but they are obsessed with *thinking* about it.

I recently talked with a client at a treatment center who spent too much time and money on the Internet, watching porno movie after porno movie—and he did nothing but watch. He also paid money for prostitutes to come to his house, and he paid them solely to masturbate while he watched.

He said that he always felt guilty and ashamed. He felt he was unable to have a real relationship. He had been involved in this aspect of sex addiction for over twenty years. However, when we spoke, he was receiving treatment. He felt confident and was enjoying the identification he was making in the support groups he attended.

*Today I will not use other people
for my personal gratification.*

God

My God today is a happy God. This helps to keep me happy.

When I was a young man I didn't see many happy faces in my church—religion was serious business! I also noticed that the sanctuary displayed many crucifixes and icons of saints who were suffering. John the Baptist was holding his head, and St. Sebastian was struggling with arrows in his body. I never saw a laughing Jesus!

This is not my church today. As a Unity minister, I see many pictures of a laughing, happy Jesus, and the worship is based upon positive and creative affirmations. We do not negate suffering, but we do not dwell on it. Our God is a happy God, and this encourages me to be happy.

I've always suggested that people worship where they feel comfortable. Some people in recovery return to the church of their childhood, and that's okay. Others, like me, find a new and different spiritual home, and that's okay, too.

I affirm a happy and joyful
Creator who loves me.

Sleep Sex

I become aggressive sexually with my wife when I am sleeping. Because of this continuing behavior, our marriage is on the brink of divorce. Then I read about sleep sex. Is this just a convenient excuse for a man with a sex addiction?

It is certainly possible for a person suffering from "sleep sex" (sexsomnia) to also be a sexual compulsive. That does not mean that sexsomnia is not an issue that must be dealt with medically. Therapy and treatment will probably be required.

I have discovered that people who are interested in spirituality usually believe that medicine and science are also involved. For many years, recovery from alcoholism has been based upon a spiritual program. This is proving to be necessary for the sexually compulsive person and could include those suffering from other sex addictions.

I believe a spiritual approach to sexsomnia will require an open mind and willingness to try new techniques in medical therapy.

Today I approach my recovery program with an open mind.

Recovery

*The 12 Step program for sex addicts is
helping me confront my denial.*

It is usually the diseases that involve shame that are the toughest to confront or accept. Alcoholism, bulimia, HIV, and AIDS, and—most certainly—sexual compulsions are, for most people, enveloped in denial.

The sufferers of such sicknesses have often been seen as weak, irresponsible, dirty, sinners, lazy, evil—not good people! When uttered by parents, church, or society in general, such condemnations have created toxic feelings of guilt and shame. Today, in some circles, such patients are still judged and condemned.

Science, medicine, and therapy are slowly breaking down these judgmental attitudes, opening the door to compassion and healing. We must add to this list self-support groups that are based upon the powerful dynamic of a person with the problem sharing honestly with another person who has the same problem. The healing derived from such a dynamic has been miraculous.

*I offer my denial, in therapy,
to my loving God.*

Exhibitionism

I go to busy restrooms and let men look at my erect penis. Occasionally, I'll masturbate. I've been arrested twice, but I continue to do it.

The person who shared this behavior with me did not believe he was gay. He was not interested in looking at other men; he enjoyed them looking at him. He was an exhibitionist. He had girlfriends do the same. He was obsessed with his own penis, and he wanted to share it with as many people as possible.

I met him when he was a patient in a treatment center for sex addiction. Before treatment he would say, "I cannot stop doing it. When the feelings arise, I expose myself."

Spiritually, people change. Maybe a better way to say this is that if someone really wants to change, then he or she can. The person might need therapy, or support, certainly encouragement—but addicts and compulsives can change their attitudes about themselves and their personal behavior.

The power of choice is spiritual.

Sexual Sobriety

What is sexual sobriety?

For the alcoholic, *sobriety* means more than simply not drinking alcohol. It also stresses the need for balance in all areas of our lives. *Abstinence* is the word for simply not drinking.

In a similar sense, *sexual sobriety* implies the need for a healthy balance concerning relationships and sexual expression. The specific manifestations of an individual's sex addiction will determine what will be involved in creating and maintaining sexual sobriety. It also will involve developing an understanding of spirituality that embraces kindness, gentleness, honesty, discipline, and rigorous boundaries.

With the help of a sponsor (who advises and guides the addict) or a therapist, the sex addict will begin a healthy spiritual journey that will bring an acceptance of his or her sex addiction and the will to live one day at a time.

My sexual sobriety requires the
attainment of balance on a daily basis.

Honesty

I've been in a lesbian relationship for seven years, but I've never been faithful. I always feel guilty about being discovered.

Cheating is one way of being dishonest. Usually, because of the shame and guilt most people feel concerning sex, covert behavior and unhealthy secrets surround the behavior. Dishonesty thrives in covert actions and secrecy. Because of the shame and low self-esteem this behavior creates, most sex addicts are not getting help or experiencing recovery.

Spirituality has become the foundation for most treatment and recovery programs addressing addiction, including sex addiction, and honesty is an essential value in sustained healing.

The honesty starts with a person sharing what is really going on in his or her life. This usually begins with a therapist. Then the addict moves on to being honest within a support group. At the right time, the addict is honest with his or her significant other, who surely has a right to know what is going on.

My spiritual growth is based upon being honest.

Secrecy

I go to a popular nudist beach to spy on people.
I watch them and secretly masturbate.
It's become an obsession.

Addicts do strange things, and spying behaviors are also dangerous. Being a Peeping Tom—a voyeur—can have severe and embarrassing legal consequences. It is also abusive to the people being spied upon and used.

We see powerlessness and unmanageability again in the preceding quotation—"It's become an obsession"—and this secret behavior creates secret shame.

Is help available? Yes. People who suffer from sexually compulsive behavior can change their lives by moving toward the spiritual attributes of respect and establishing firm and healthy boundaries. With a program of recovery for sex addiction, the acting out diminishes progressively and spiritual wellness is attained—one day at a time.

I affirm that people can change their
destructive and abusive behavior.

The Game

I know I'm a sex addict. And I really get off on the secret aspect of my behavior. It's like a game, and my family has to catch me.

A symptom of sex addiction that is rarely discussed is the adrenaline rush, the euphoria that accompanies the secrecy. The covert behaviors that are designed to keep the family and loved ones ignorant are indeed a game:

- Will they catch me?
- I've come so close to being discovered at my computer.
- My girlfriend left before my wife returned from work, and my wife suspects nothing.
- I was masturbating while I spoke with my husband on the telephone. He thought I was happy to talk with him.
- I discreetly touched the neighbor's kid at the dinner table. The child said nothing.

We confront and progressively terminate the sick game by healthy disclosure.

I am willing to surrender my secrets in the hope of healing.

Inappropriate Behavior

I think my husband is inappropriate with the grandchildren. He touches and kisses them too much. But I don't know how to talk to him.

We've heard this many times: A family member does not know how to begin the conversation concerning sex addiction. It is too embarrassing. It is too personal. It often appears as if the significant other has absorbed the sex addict's shame.

I trust the instinct of the wife in the preceding quotation. When she says, "He touches and kisses them too much," a serious boundary issue is going on, if not a more serious behavior.

The spiritual healing for the sexual compulsive or sex addict is when the spouse is able to break the silence, beginning to share his or her concerns with somebody trustworthy, possibly a therapist or social worker.

The consequences of not sharing feelings can be tragic for all concerned.

I pray for courage as I confront inappropriate behavior.

Sex Addiction

I know sleeping with a married man is not good for me. It goes against all my moral convictions, but I love the sex.

When we talk about being sexually compulsive—balance is lacking, and the sexual behavior is addictive and obsessive—it is important to emphasize the word *compulsive*. Because of this, the addict says, "It goes against all my moral convictions."

St. Paul said in Romans 7:19, "For what I do is not the good I want to do; no, the evil I do not want to do—this I keep doing." This is the paradoxical tragedy of living with addictive behavior, including sexual compulsivity.

The pain must outweigh the pleasure for healing to begin. Also, the unmanageability being experienced and the powerlessness being felt must prompt action. Help is available. Sex addicts are rebuilding their lives. The spiritual program is providing healing for families that were falling apart. Balance and serenity are being experienced.

I'm seeking to reclaim my moral high ground.

Forgiveness

Jesus said, "Forgive them for they know not what they do."

—*Luke 23:34*

I've preached many sermons on this text, believed to be among the last words that Jesus spoke from the cross before he died.

How do these words apply to the sex addict? Well, during my time as a spiritual advisor to treatment centers that treat sex addiction, I've heard many tragic and depressing stories, some of them involving children and animals. Some self-righteous people often feel disgusted, judging that the best recipe for such addicts is prison and throwing away the key!

I've never had these feelings. I know what it is to do things that are wrong, and the awareness of my faults has created a bridge to the most damaged sex addict.

I forgive because I have
been forgiven.

Abuse

I followed a young girl in the mall. When she looked at me, I rubbed my crotch. I want to do it again, and yet I feel guilty.

I've heard stories like this in support groups for years. However, some things are really hard to talk about. More than shameful, they feel disgusting, even exploitative of children. Are sex addicts monsters? No. But some people, because of their ignorance and perfectionism, backed up at times by religious texts, often have made it appear so.

Sex addiction, when it consumes all your thoughts and actions, makes you do and say things you would never normally do or say. Unhealthy shame and holier-than-thou judgments are not helpful. Responsibility, change, forgiveness, and healing can only come in the form of experiencing spirituality and a therapy that brings hope.

There but by the grace of God go I.
Amen.

Resurrection

In recovery I've experienced a new life. I'm a Christian, and it's like experiencing resurrection.

Spirituality is different from religion, and I know spiritual people who will live their lives without ever going to a church or temple. They've found a Higher Power in the living of their lives.

I've also met people who, after treatment, went back to their church with "a new pair of spectacles." They return with a deeper appreciation of the Scriptures and a new love of the liturgy. In the preceding quotation we hear about a Christian, but it is also true for Muslims, Jews, Buddhists, Hindus, and others.

God has always been found in religion, and some religious people who have been sainted in our time teach love, tolerance, and forgiveness. Recovery from addiction is a form of resurrection, coming back from the old life to live the new life.

I am reborn in my recovery.

Spirituality

What is a spiritual healing for a sex addiction?
Does it mean I must go to a church?

Spirituality and religion are different. We rarely choose our religion. Most people who are Christian come from Christian parents, most Jews come from Jewish parents, and so on—and only a few people change their religion. It is my belief that spirituality is a choice. It is the acceptance of paths to God other than the one into which we were born, and these "spiritual paths" may be religious or not.

My spiritual program involves worshiping at a church, but I'm also comfortable attending a Native American meeting or a Jewish synagogue. To answer the question asked in the preceding quotation, spiritual healing does not mean that you *must* go to church. Spiritual healing is not connected with any one religion or denomination: Each person is free to discover it in their own particular way.

I've discovered a spiritual healing that
runs deep within nature itself.

Exploitation

My daughter found my hidden camera in the bathroom. She became hysterical when she realized I'd filmed the grandchildren. I worry that she might report me.

Sex addiction takes us into some dark places. I'm reminded that in movies I've seen about Dr. Jekyll and Mr. Hyde, the gentlemanly Dr. Jekyll becomes a creature of the night when he changes into Mr. Hyde. Dr. Jekyll is respectful and charming with women; Mr. Hyde is cruel and exploitative. A case for sex addiction could certainly be made after a consideration of Mr. Hyde's behaviors.

Sex addicts exploit people, occasionally even their grandchildren. When children's privacy has been desecrated, the feelings of shame, guilt, violence, disgust, anger, and despair can become intermingled—and yes, the law should be involved.

Help often comes at the price of social freedom!

My fears and shame I bring to God.
Today I cannot forgive myself.
I trust that God can.

The Unspeakable

I get sexually excited when I masturbate my dog. Is something wrong with me?

Yes, something is wrong. The person asking if something is wrong is probably secretive and ashamed. This behavior is also abusive to the dog.

Sexual activity involving animals is not uncommon with certain sex addicts, and it reflects, in an extreme form, obsessive and compulsive thoughts about sex. I can only imagine the issues of shame, low self-esteem, and self-loathing: How do you talk openly about such behavior? Even to read it is embarrassing.

We must remember that such behavior is a demonstration of sickness. And yet, help is available. Many people who have abused animals are recovering. The essential spiritual hurdle is overcome when the person is willing to talk about it.

I am willing to speak honestly about behavior
I was raised to consider unspeakable.

A Miracle

The Twelve Step programs, which are helping those suffering from all addictions, are a miracle from God.

Over the years I've heard people describe many things as miracles, but it is not often that I hear the 12 Step program described as one. But it is. Millions of people, in a variety of 12 Step programs that address issues concerning alcohol, drugs, gambling, food, and sex, are getting help on a daily basis. This program also extends to family members and friends.

For some, the miracle is found in people with a problem talking to people who also have that problem. And it's not always the person with many years of recovery talking to the newcomer—sometimes the newcomer helps the newcomer.

The miracle is also found in knowing that we are not alone, that we will not be judged. The miracle is manifest in accepting our humanity.

My imperfections are a bridge to the imperfections of another.

Violation

I have been dating a man for six months, and my teenage daughter says he is inappropriate with her when they hug. He likes to tickle her. Should I say something?

Sexual compulsivity often reveals itself in unhealthy boundary issues. It is always unacceptable behavior, and when a teenager feels he or she is being treated inappropriately, it indicates that something is seriously wrong. To tickle a teenager against her wishes is abusive, and something should be said and done.

A mother who asks permission to say something about inappropriate behavior is obviously not a completely healthy person. We see similar behavior in lovers of alcoholics, and it indicates that self-esteem issues and neediness are affecting judgment.

Therapy is required in such cases: certainly for the couple and possibly also for the teenager. If an intervention does not take place quickly, the inappropriate behavior will become progressively more exploitative.

When I see abuse, I will speak out.

Prejudice

I'm a gay man who was shamed by the condemnations I heard in my fundamentalist church. Today I understand that spirituality is not religion.

All religions have, at times, hurt people with judgments and condemnations. Gays and lesbians have often been particularly singled out, and many had to leave their religion of birth.

Spirituality is less dogmatic, less black-and-white. It refers to the poets as easily as to sacred writings. It affirms that many paths lead to God and that all religions are evaluated with respect. Indeed, it is my belief that a person can embrace spirituality without having to believe in God.

In addition, it is important for therapists and treatment centers to acknowledge the damage created by religious abuse and to include this initial information in their approach to sex addiction.

I understand the difference between my childhood fundamentalism and spirituality.

Consequences

I'm facing sexual assault charges. Maybe I'll go to prison. I've been sexually compulsive since being a young man. An uncle had sex with me when I was nine, and that was about the time I began acting out sexually.

It is interesting to note the number of sex addicts who were traumatized or sexually abused as children. Is this why they are addicts? Well, it may not be the *only* reason, but it probably played an important role. What is clear is that abuse, or trauma, always has an effect on a person, particularly a young person.

Some sex addicts grew up in homes where sex was not mentioned. Others heard religious preachers condemn most sexual behavior to hell, and yet saw television and newspaper advertisements that showed pictures of nearly naked women and men used to sell their products—all confusing, yet enticing.

The spiritual solution is focused not so much on what made us sex addicts but what we are willing *to do* about it. Spirituality always teaches personal responsibility.

I respect the power of sex.

Love Addiction

What is love addiction?

Recently psychologists and psychiatrists have been focusing on an aspect of codependency: that excessive neediness affects loving relationships. Because of the compulsivity involved, they have coined the term *love addiction*. I've also heard the expression *romance addiction*.

This addiction is often an adult relationship without an emphasis upon sex. Certainly, sex is not the driving force for love addicts; rather it is the desperate search for romance, to feel wanted, to be needed. It is not unusual for love addicts to find themselves in a relationship with a sex addict, and then they willingly exchange sex to maintain the relationship. They are willing to exchange sex for love.

Rarely are love addicts able to verbalize, without therapy, what they feel is happening to them. They tend to wallow in guilt and shame until they get help. A healthy observer sees clearly that it is their excessive neediness that is creating most of the problem.

I affirm the establishment of healthy boundaries in my loving relationships.

Change

Can you recover from sex addiction by praying to God?

I would never doubt or discourage the significance of prayer in any person's life. Prayer is powerful. Prayer often brings about the changes that lead to a miracle. As a powerful agent between a person and his or her God, prayer should never be marginalized.

Spiritually, however, I tend to see prayer as an opening to change. It is that important time, before the action, when we focus, in the Divine Presence, on what must be done.

Most sex addicts pray, and most are praying about the shame that surrounds their behaviors as sex addicts. It has been my experience that they pray often, but recovery comes with action.

Knowing that the Divine Healer works through therapy, they get up from their knees and walk toward the therapeutic couch.

I pray, and then I move my feet
in the direction of recovery.

Questions

I have sex as often as possible. Everyone does.
Or do they? Am I becoming a sex addict?

The awareness that you have an addiction is often preceded by an uncomfortable feeling about your behavior. A person begins to question if they are acting differently from others, wondering if they have crossed that invisible line that makes them an addict.

I did this with my alcoholism. I used to say that everybody likes to drink, that most people get drunk on weekends, everyone must wind down, a little drink hurts nobody, you'd drink if you did the work that I do.

These generalizations were all excuses. I was uncomfortable with my drinking, but I didn't want to say I had a problem.

The hope for recovery is seen in the question *"Or do they?"* Everyone is *not* having sex during spring break. Everyone is *not* having irresponsible sex. And more important, everyone is *not* asking if he or she is a sex addict.

Spiritually, I understand that feeling
uncomfortable with my behavior
often leads to healthy changes.

Facing the Issues

I am a sex addict and an alcoholic. Can I just go to my AA meetings?

Indeed, many alcoholics who are also sex addicts do go only to their AA meetings. Some do not know or are in denial of their sex addiction, but they have accepted their alcoholism and seek support from other recovering alcoholics.

The spiritual power of recovery is usually seen in a person with a particular problem sharing with other people who have the same problem. AA meetings are not the place to discuss sex addiction or to obtain helpful insights into a recovery plan for sex addiction. Therefore, I recommend that any sex addict who is also alcoholic go to both sex addiction and alcoholism support groups. I believe we feel spiritually safe when we discuss issues or behaviors that resonate with others at a meeting.

I seek God's message of healing in the people with whom I can identify.

Low Self–Esteem

My self-esteem is real low except when it comes to sex. People say I'm real good at it. So that's what I do.

I know some people who were sexually abused as children and therefore learned about sexual practices at an early age. They were given the message that their value as a human being was dependent upon their ability to deliver sex. That was what pleased their abuser. That was what they felt they were good at doing. Their self-worth and self-esteem were related to their sexual expression.

While growing up in this dysfunctional environment, their main focus in life was sex, and they may have felt inferior in other social interactions. I remember a person in treatment saying, "Sex is who I am."

Spiritually, this is not true, and it *never* was true. The process of healing will require replacing the old self-talk with new internal messages that stress personality, expressing healthy feelings, and confidence in the ability to change behaviors.

*I am not what I learned
in my childhood.*

Reality

I am a sex addict, but I don't hurt anyone.
What I do is in private.

When I quote "Love God and your neighbor as yourself" (Matthew 22:36-39) to an audience, people often look at me in amazement. They know the quote, but they rarely have applied it to a love of self. Indeed, I go further and say that if you really want to love God and your neighbor it is *essential* that you learn to love yourself.

I want people to realize how important it is to have a love and respect for themselves.

In the preceding quotation, we see that this particular sex addict does not see that the someone he is hurting is himself. This isolating behavior keeps the sex addict from mixing in a healthy way with others to form loving and creative relationships.

Such isolating behavior causes us all to lose.

My love of self is helping me
heal my sex addiction.

Odd Behavior

I read about a man who had sex with chickens. I often think about this and masturbate. Do you think I'll try to do it?

Wnen a client shared this story with me, I didn't believe him. First, how could a man have sex with a chicken? Also, why would somebody find it sexually stimulating? It seemed fantastical.

Then I remembered my stories as an alcoholic: falling into the grave while still saying the prayers, baptizing a little boy with a girl's name. Crazy. Fantastical. Then I remembered countless stories I'd heard from other addicts, gamblers, compulsive eaters—many incredible. Always crazy—fantastical.

Sex addiction takes you into a fantastical world of sexual compulsivity and theater. Why not chickens? What surely elicits hope is that the person asking the question about chickens was in treatment.

I understand that spirituality connects with therapy.

Judgment

I love my wife, but I hate her sex addiction. I feel so ashamed of her, and I worry about our children.

ew illnesses, if any, carry the shame of sex addiction. Alcoholism, drug addiction, and bulimia are close, but because of religious teachings—the morality lessons that so many of us received concerning sexuality while growing up—nothing quite compares with sex addiction. Most people heard the following remarks during childhood:

- Sex is sinful outside of marriage.
- Masturbation will make you blind and send you to hell.
- Sex was created to produce children.
- Only whores and reprobates enjoy sex.
- Sex destroyed our paradise in the Garden of Eden.

For these reasons, a critical aspect of healing the sex addict involves spiritual healing. We must learn to talk about sex without feeling ashamed, or guilty.

I'm discovering that my hatreds reveal the parts of myself I cannot accept.

Denial

I told my girlfriend that I am a sex addict.
She laughed. But she does not know what I do
when I'm not with her.

Most people laugh nervously when sex issues are mentioned. When I've referred to sex addiction during a lecture, people in the audience have chuckled. However, sex addiction is not a laughing matter, especially when we know the real symptoms of sex addiction and the behaviors.

From the preceding quote, neither we nor the addict's girlfriend can know the person's sex addiction. Is it compulsive masturbation? Does he use pornography and the Internet, prostitutes, girlie bars? We simply do not know. That is why the girlfriend was able to laugh.

I congratulate the fact that this man is beginning to talk about his sickness, and I hope he involves himself with a support group or therapy. If he does, he eventually will be able to get his girlfriend to understand the pain and shame of his addiction.

My therapy is helping me understand that
sex addiction is not a laughing matter.

Making Amends

*In my recovery program, I sometimes must make
amends to those I've hurt or exploited sexually.
I'm amazed at the many people who are pleased
I made my amends and am now in recovery.*

This is a clear reference to the following tenets of the
12 Step program:

- Step 4: Made a searching and fearless moral inventory of ourselves.
- Step 5: Admitted to God, to ourselves, and to another human being the exact nature of our wrongs.
- Step 6: Were entirely ready to have God remove all these defects of character.
- Step 7: Humbly asked God to remove our shortcomings.
- Step 8: Made a list of all persons we had harmed, and became willing to make amends to them all.

The majority of people who are aware of their own
imperfections will forgive the imperfections of others.

*My spiritual program teaches me to make
amends promptly when I am wrong.*

Unhealthy

My eight-year-old son is inappropriate with his sister. He's too sexual.

If a parent feels that a son is being inappropriate with his sister, especially in a sexual way, then something must be said, something must be done. It must not be ignored or denied.

This behavior could be the beginning of sex addiction, but it is too early to put labels on any child, especially sexual labels that could create shame and covert behavior in the teenage years. However, I've heard young people share at alcoholism support meetings that their alcoholism was apparent at a very young age. Sexual compulsivity can also reveal itself at a young age.

It is best to begin the conversation that involves healthy boundaries and respect than to ignore the subject. If inappropriate activity does not subside, then see a therapist who specializes in nurturing healthy behavior in young children.

*The spiritual value of respect must
be taught at a young age.*

Relapse

I was in recovery from sex addiction for two years when I went to see a regular movie, but it was rated "R" and had explicit sex scenes. I relapsed.

I remember a cocaine addict sharing with me that while having coffee with friends someone accidentally spilled some sweetener on the table. Nobody noticed the white powder—*except him*. He could not take his eyes off it, and his thoughts became obsessed with cocaine. Later that evening he relapsed.

Many triggers go unnoticed by the ordinary person but become the gateway back to an addiction. In the preceding quotation, we see how a regular R-rated movie triggered a person's sex addiction.

For this reason, therapists stress the need for personal boundaries. Addicts should avoid people and situations that are connected with their *individual* addictive behavior. Rigorous honesty will help avoid slippery situations.

My spiritual program insists that I practice rigorous honesty to avoid potential disasters.

Cheating

I've cheated on my wife for years. I've had many women. Does that make me a sex addict?

I've often been asked the question, "If I drink six beers a day, am I an alcoholic?" It is not for me, or anyone else, to say who is an alcoholic. This is also true regarding sex addiction. I will share what sex addiction looks like and will ask you to decide.

Cheats rarely feel good about cheating. Being dishonest and telling lies to a wife, and presumably to other women, hardly characterizes the behavior of a noble person. Because of the associated covert behavior and sustained manipulation, sex addiction does not make sex addicts feel good about themselves. Most feel guilty and ashamed.

Feeling badly about your sexual behaviors probably leads to covert behavior. Then you discover what you are doing and that you are becoming what you do not like, and you are not proud of such behaviors. That's sex addiction.

I once was lost.
Now I'm on the journey to self-respect.

Sex Addiction

*I'm so shy I need alcohol to have sex. I'll even
take drugs. But sex is what I want.*

When I go to support meetings for recovering alcoholics, I hear people talking about feeling "less
than," about their low self-esteem issues, and about never
feeling good enough. Low self-esteem has become, for
many treatment centers, a symptom of alcoholism.

These same feelings are often expressed by a person
who has a sex addiction. In the preceding quotation, we
see that feeling shy prompts the use of alcohol or drugs,
but the real intention is to have sex.

The fascination with wanting sex, almost an obsession, has led to dangerous and illegal behaviors. These
are red flags!

Spiritually, the key to healing this behavior is for the
person to seek help. Therapy will probably be necessary.

*I've moved from talking
about my problem to doing
something about it.*

Irresponsibility

My spring break lasts a year. The adventures of spring break are my life!

Most parents worry about what could happen to their children at spring break. Teachers and social workers are often seen on television talking about the dangerous spring break escapades in which teenagers indulge. Drugs, alcohol, and sex are their main concerns.

The addict is attracted to euphoric behavior, experiencing "a high," feeding the pleasure zones in the brain. These desires are some of the symptoms one often sees in the young, especially teenagers. Can teenagers be sex addicts? They certainly can, in the same way that they can be compulsive about alcohol, drugs, and food. The challenge is in owning sexually addictive behavior alongside the degree of fear and shame associated with sex.

The spring break season tends to open a Pandora's box, and for a short period of time people are concerned—then the denial returns.

I'm realizing, as I mature, that not everything that feels good is good!

Faith

I was recently "born again." I believe that in Jesus I am healed.

I don't deny that many people are "born again" into the healing power of Jesus, and this provides a powerful foundation for spiritual transformation. However, that does not mean that God is not at work in other groups and agencies other than a church or prayer group.

Consider the number of Christians, "born again" or not, who seek the medical help of doctors, dentists, and ophthalmologists because their personal health is helped by these medical professionals. I believe that sex addicts are helped in a similar way by psychiatrists, psychologists, therapists, and Sex Addicts Anonymous (SAA) support groups.

When Jesus said that he was present where two or three are gathered together, he did not specify a church gathering!

I hear the power of God's spoken word in the honest sharing at my support group.

Sexualization

*I'm often inappropriate when I look at people.
I stare at their breasts, crotch, and lips. It causes
regular arguments with my wife. But I can't stop.*

Our internal voice does not always speak the truth, no matter how many times the messages are repeated.

If we keep believing that we cannot change, then assuredly we will not. People have said, "I cannot stop smoking, using alcohol, taking drugs, eating." And now we hear that a person is unable to change inappropriate behavior.

These statements are untrue. We *can* change. People are recovering from sex addiction and sexual compulsivity in growing numbers. A key spiritual ingredient is beginning to change the message that we play in our heads, mainly from "I cannot" to "Today I will."

Recovery begins with the way we think about what we can do.

*I no longer accept my past excuses
for inappropriate behavior.*

Honesty

I'm a priest. I'm also an untreated alcoholic and sex addict. Who can I tell?

It is sad that this priest feels so alone. Yet many clergy, who live lives that are engaged in helping others, are seemingly incapable of asking for help for themselves. This is not unique to clergy. Most professionals in mental health services, who are excellent at giving advice to others, rarely seek help for themselves. Perhaps some believe that because they are immersed in health-care services they will receive healing by osmosis!

However, help is available. Most religious denominations are aware of the growing number of alcoholics, drug addicts, and, yes, sex addicts in their congregations—and help is also available for clergy. Clergy have friends. Clergy can see doctors and therapists. Most clergy are aware of the 12 Step programs that support addicts.

Maybe unhealthy pride is prompting the priest's question?

Today I know I'm a healer
in need of healing.

Violence

*I use a sex toy to hurt my girlfriend. I know
she hates me doing it, but I force her. Then I
feel ashamed.*

We have read in these pages that partners of sex
addicts are abused. In the situation quoted here,
the abuse involves violent behavior.

Alongside the question, "Why is he hurting his girlfriend?" is the question, "Why does she put up with it?"
This obviously is an unhealthy relationship. Both partners will need therapy.

This type of unhealthy relationship is not unusual for
the sex addicted. Some people enjoy hurting others
(sadism), and others prefer, consciously or subcon-
sciously, to be hurt (masochism). Feelings of guilt and
shame invariably follow, but the abuse usually continues
until one partner or both seek help.

The relationship presented here obviously lacks respect.
Can he change? Absolutely. Can she change? Yes. But
long-term help from a professional is required.

*I seek to embrace respect in
all that I do and say.*

Obsessive

I go to sex addiction support groups to pick up men. I wonder if I'm a sex addict.

This person must know something about sex addiction to know where to find the sex addiction support groups. She is trying to have her sexual needs met by people who are confessed sex addicts. It's not for me to say who is a sex addict, but I remember this: "If it walks like a duck, looks like a duck, quacks like a duck, it probably is a duck."

A friend once told me, while we were discussing alcoholism, that ordinary people who drink alcohol rarely ask themselves if they are alcoholic. I've usually discovered that alcoholics, before they admit to being alcoholic, ask, "I wonder if I'm an alcoholic?" This is also true with sex addiction.

> *My God of Truth demands*
> *that I get honest.*

Sexsomnia

*This week my fiancé woke me four times during
the night. He had put his hand down my panties
and was stroking my vagina and rectum.
He had no recollection of doing this.*

The power of sexuality is such that it can follow us
into our sleep, and according to research that has
been done by Simone O'Gorman and others, it constitutes the medical disorder named *sexsomnia*. The Internet contains enough information for us to know that
many people, not unlike the woman in the preceding
quotation, wake in the night to find their partner having
sex or making sexual advances while asleep. The next
morning, or upon awakening, they do not recall their
sexual behavior.

Is sexsomnia an aspect of sex addiction? I'm not sure.
Certainly sex addicts have used the "sleep" excuse to
avoid taking responsibility for their sexual behavior.
Research is ongoing, but what we do know is that the
sex urge for some is overwhelming and does affect some
people in their sleep.

I respectfully fear the power of sex in my life.

Connection

Going to meetings helps me realize I'm not alone.

I've heard that the fastest-growing 12 Step meetings in the United States concern sex addiction. The sickness is coming out of the shadows. More people than ever before are recognizing when they have a sexual compulsion, love addiction, or sex addiction. The behavior is being discussed as a serious relapse issue by alcohol and drug counselors. And yes, help is definitely on the way!

Because loneliness—a key issue with any addiction, particularly sex addiction—is so difficult to talk about, surrounded by guilt and shame, the sex addict feels isolated and alone. As the preceding quotation reveals, going to meetings and sitting with people who are facing similar problems help to break down those feelings of separateness. *I'm not alone.*

In meetings,
I find my spiritual center.

Intervention

Ten years ago my mother confronted me about my constant use of pornography in magazines and on the Internet. Now I'm in recovery, and I thank God for my mother's intervention.

I had a wonderful mother. She helped me get into recovery for my alcoholism. My mother said to me, "Leo, I love you enough to let you go. If you don't get help, I will ask you to leave my house, and I will not support you with money or excuses." In 1977 this was strong stuff—and it is still potent!

A mother's role is special in a family. She often must practice "tough love" with all the family, including a sexually addicted son.

Maybe in the context of the preceding quotation, what I've said many times about my mother applies: "She said what she meant and meant what she said."

*Today, as I remember my mother,
I seek to reflect her spirituality
in my own life.*

Binge Sex

I go on sexual binges. That was how I used to drink before getting into recovery. With sex I can get "lost" for weeks in sexual cravings, and then I have a dry spell.

When discussing addiction, health professionals often refer to *cross-addiction*, which is present when a person has more than one compulsive behavior.

For years in support groups for alcoholics, we were aware of compulsive sexual behavior, but we didn't call it an addiction. Instead, we said that such a person, if male, was "a player." However, addiction is addiction, and many therapists are suggesting that sex addiction has symptoms and relationship challenges comparable to those of alcoholism. These addictions often coexist.

The recovery process for alcoholism and for sex addiction is the same: Admit the problem, seek help, develop a spiritual program.

As a recovering alcoholic, I am not alone with having a sex addiction.

Forgiveness

I'm understanding that forgiveness is a process.
Healing from my sex addiction requires forgiveness.

We have discussed throughout this book that sex addiction creates in the individual and family tremendous guilt and shame. Sex, outside of marriage, was often seen to be sinful, making the sex addict feel *unforgivable*.

While I do not believe this to be true—nobody should be cast aside as being worthless—sex addicts, alongside other addicts, must take some responsibility for past behavior on their journey toward recovery and healing. Forgiveness requires not only change but also *ownership*.

The process of forgiveness is a powerful gift that requires a willingness to make, where appropriate, a sincere apology to those people who were hurt by our destructive and selfish behavior. *Saying* "Sorry" is the step beyond *being* sorry. Only then can we experience true freedom.

Making amends is the gift
I bestow upon myself.

Healing

Jesus has forgiven me. That's all I need.

I understand that for many Christians their relationship with Jesus is such that forgiveness and healing rest in him. I think this point of view must be respected. Yet it is not unusual for such Christians to also wear eyeglasses, have false teeth, or undergo various forms of medical implants that keep them healthy. Very few Christians reject *all* medical help.

Therapy and treatment for sex addiction constitute one aspect of medical assistance. Alongside worship in church, Bible readings, and belief in Jesus, a decisive change in behavior must occur. From the preceding quotation, we can assume that the sex addiction occurred during the person's church attendance or belief in Jesus—yet the addiction continued. And so something more must happen.

My suggestion is church, Bible reading, and therapy for a comprehensive religious and spiritual healing.

Spiritually, I understand that Jesus works through the healing concepts found in medicine.

Recovery

*I've been going to sex addiction support groups
for more than three years. It has changed my life.
I've never been so happy.*

It is important to know that people are healing and
recovering from sex addiction. Families and loved ones
are reunited, and past manipulations, deceit, and lies are
forgiven.

Is it any great surprise that many addicts cry when
they hear the hymn, "Amazing Grace," and apply it to
themselves?

Amazing grace! How sweet the sound,
That saved a wretch like me.
I once was lost but now am found,
Was blind, but now I see. . . .

Needless to say, the sex addict completely identifies
with this poetic journey into spiritual healing.

*I polish my miracle every day with
spiritual thoughts and actions.*

Ignorance

I told my boyfriend I'm a sex addict. He asked what I meant, and I told him. He called me a slut. He doesn't return my calls. I'm so ashamed.

Not everybody is ready to understand sex addiction. Indeed, many people still do not accept that alcoholism and drug addiction are treatable diseases. I remember having friends and family members tell me, "Just quit it. Know when to put the plug in the jug."

In the preceding quotation, we see that the boyfriend didn't understand, but from the abusive name he called her she is probably better off not being with him. He only reinforced her shame.

Women and men suffer from sex addiction. Because of the latent sexism that still exists in our society, women are the least understood, often receiving the greater condemnation. However, recovery and healing are attainable. Many women are in treatment and enjoying recovery one day at a time. Help is available.

I ignore the ignorance and focus on my spiritual healing.

Sex Games

I've been married to my husband for five years. He's happy with our relationship, but I encourage him to find other men and women to share our bed. I love the excitement of sex.

I've never wanted to be "the law" when it comes to the sexual behaviors some people feel they need to be satisfied or happy. Religious and sexual freedoms are important in a healthy and spiritual society.

However, it is not okay for people to hurt or take advantage of others, sexually or in any other way. At all times, children and the mentally challenged need to be protected. The preceding quotation may not be an indication of sexually addictive behavior, but it seems that a possible conflict may arise between the husband, who is happy in the marriage relationship, and the wife, who obviously seems to require more sexual encounters; she's what we would call a "swinger." For the wife, more people equal more excitement, with the emphasis on *more*, which is always a danger sign when discussing addiction.

I understand that sex involves more than excitement.

Compulsivity

I knew a nun who masturbated ten times a day.
She felt so ashamed that she eventually left the
convent. She's still a compulsive masturbator.

Sexual compulsives often feel that if they join a church or synagogue, maybe even get involved with a strict religious group, then their behavior will change, but it rarely does. I know gay men who thought that their feelings would go away if they trained for the priesthood, but the results were invariably disastrous. It is interesting that a rigid morality, which often created the covert sexual behaviors, is seen as a possible cure for those behaviors.

Anything that creates shame, guilt, or low self-esteem is a problem. In this case, it is essential for the nun to seek help and support for her compulsive masturbation. And the help is available to her in 12 Step support groups, therapists, and treatment centers that specialize in sexual compulsivity issues. Hopefully, she can break the barriers of shame and get the help she needs.

The spiritual word surrender
teaches me to ask for help.

Consequences

I never got married because I couldn't be faithful.
I'm old and lonely.

It is amazing to read about the sacrifices that some sex addicts have made in order to continue their obsessive behavior. The preceding quotation clearly reveals that marriage and being faithful in that marriage were not as important as "playing the field," during which *more sex* was substituted for *better quality* in relationships.

The result was old age and loneliness, but this need not be the "last chapter." Whatever happened in the past, wherever the untreated sex addiction took that person, it is still possible to embrace recovery and find personal healing. Even in the autumn of life, a meaningful relationship can be developed with friends who have embraced recovery. Spiritually, I've always been an optimist concerning the future.

I embrace the concept of being positive
and creative in my life.

Being Human

My bishop had to move me from my ministerial post because I had sex with a member of the congregation.

It might seem unnecessary, in the light of sexual abuse issues concerning clergy, to state that sex addiction and sexual compulsivity affect clergy alongside everyone else. But still, people have a tendency, after all the negative publicity, to place clergy on pedestals, believing that the temptations that affect ordinary people are not present in the lives of those who are "called" by God to his service.

The truth is that clergy of all denominations have the same sexual challenges and compulsions as ordinary folk. Indeed, because of the unrealistic expectations placed upon the clergy, they are more likely to engage in covert sexual behaviors that in turn trigger sex addiction.

The key to healing is not prayer alone—but also treatment.

As a member of the clergy,
I submit to therapy and healing.

Euphoria

During my lunch hour I masturbate. A girl in the office occasionally joins me. The covert behavior we engage in excites me.

Here we see a symptom of sex addiction that must be understood: the thrill and excitement that accompany the covert behavior. It is the age-old fascination with doing what is forbidden, the euphoria created by engaging in secretive behavior. This is what creates the accompanying "high."

Sex addicts enjoy company, and they seek it out, in this instance, with a coworker.

As long as the behavior is felt to be exciting, with no negative consequences, it probably will continue. Healing usually begins when consequences resulting from this behavior are felt. My suspicion in response to the preceding quotation is that it's only a matter of time. Crazy and unhealthy behavior tends to precede the intervention that offers the necessary help.

*I appreciate the painful intervention
that created my spiritual healing.*

Enjoyment

I don't have to go to SAA; rather, I want to go to meetings.

A therapist shared this thought with me recently, and I could really identify: I don't *have* to go to support meetings for alcoholics; I *want* to go to my meetings. It is true that recovery is something that we need to work on, possibly every day, but it brings with it manifold gifts that far exceed the work involved.

- When I go to meetings, I'm around friends.
- They share my thoughts, doubts, and feelings.
- Their stories concerning alcoholism, mingled with laughter, I have experienced.
- The word *meetings* does not do justice to what I find there; I meet my second family: the family that really understands me.

I'm convinced that the sex addicts who get involved in support meetings will find friendship, a safe place to share, and laughter.

*My support group has become
my spiritual family.*

Questions

I like men and women. I have sex with both.
Am I a sex addict?

A bisexual person is not necessarily a sex addict any more than a heterosexual or homosexual person is a sex addict. He or she could be a sex addict—but no more than people oriented sexually in any other way.

Sex addiction is experienced when a consistent pattern of obsessiveness is linked directly to sexual thoughts or expressions. Addiction is not about *liking something;* rather, it is about uncontrollable urges that, if left untreated, create disaster.

The spiritual program seeks to bring balance and healthy boundaries to the sex addict. Based upon the spiritual formula of becoming a positive and creative person, the sex addict seeks to confront unhealthy behaviors before they create disaster and despair.

Concerning the preceding quotation, being bisexual is not indicative of a psychiatric disorder, but having a sex addiction is.

I seek a spiritual expression
for my bisexuality.

Unhealthy Thoughts

My sex addiction is not active. I do not behave sexually, but I think about it often. I seem to sexualize everyone I meet.

Sex addiction is not only about what you do. It is not connected or restricted to a *performance behavior*. Indeed, many sex addicts are consumed with *unhealthy thoughts* that are never expressed, that persist in destroying a person from the inside.

It would be a mistake to think that because you are not actively doing something—for example, masturbating, attending swinger clubs, searching for pornography on the Internet, using prostitutes—that your sex addiction is not active. Thoughts alone can destroy. Sickly thoughts can affect a relationship or family. Thoughts alone can lead to despair.

I would suggest that a person who is consumed by unhealthy sexual thoughts seek out help through a 12 Step support group and a therapist. To be consumed by sexualized thinking makes the sickness active.

Today I understand that my thinking determines my eventual behavior.

Honesty

I enjoy being a sex addict.

It is really difficult to believe that a person enjoys being an addict. Addiction is not something to celebrate.

However, maybe such a person has not yet experienced the powerlessness and unmanageability that inevitably accompany addiction, the guilt and shame created by a sexual behavior that is out of control, the embarrassment of family and friends discovering where a sex addiction has led.

Remember, addiction is a *lack of balance*. It involves an obsessiveness and compulsiveness that indicate a "mental sickness," a behavior concerning sex that is occasionally out of control. This is different from healthy and regular sexual expression.

Thank you, Great Spirit,
for the gift of reality that enables
me to overcome my denial.

Awareness

*I caught my daughter masturbating. She's only
ten. Could she be a sex addict?*

Because we are hearing and reading more about sex
addiction than ever before, it is easy to jump to the
conclusion, when we experience a sexual act, we tend to
connect it to sex addiction.

Masturbation is not uncommon in young children. It
can be a healthy aspect of the child becoming comfortable with his or her body and exploring those aspects of
touch that feel good and pleasurable. Obviously, if a parent feels that the activity is happening too often or in
inappropriate situations, then a gentle and supportive
conversation must take place. A child must know when
self-touching is inappropriate. If the parent continues to
be concerned, a pediatrician should be consulted.

*Spiritually, I'm grateful that
sex can be discussed without feeling
shame or embarrassment.*

Obsession

*A woman flashed me on the freeway. I followed
her twenty miles—but eventually came home.
Do I have a problem?*

The woman certainly has a problem. It is socially dangerous and sexually exploitative to flash a stranger, especially on a freeway!

"Do I have a problem?" Yes, this person has a problem, in that he followed her for twenty miles. I wonder, was he looking inappropriately at passing cars (staring) hoping to be flashed?

Alcoholics Anonymous describes addiction as "cunning, baffling, and powerful." This is also true for sex addiction. Few professionals think it helpful to tell a person that he or she is a sex addict; rather, it is something that must be decided by oneself.

Sex addiction is a profound loss of control that will eventually create havoc in personal and social relationships—and chasing a stranger for twenty miles doesn't seem healthy!

*I seek a spiritual program that helps
me heal my compulsive urges.*

Sex Talk

I love to hear sex talk. I spend too much money calling "phone sex" lines. I don't want to do anything except listen.

When a person says, "I don't want to do anything except listen," that's still *doing* something!

Many people think that the sex addiction referenced in the preceding quotation is about physically having sex. However, many sex addicts are involved in voyeurism or listening to phone sex.

A possible indication of sex addiction is the expression, "I *love* to hear sex talk." The word *love* seems over the top, indicating a lack of balance.

It is generally agreed by professionals that a spiritual program helps addicts affirm the need for serenity and balance in all areas of life, thereby reducing the feelings of guilt and shame.

Today I seek to affirm in my life that peace that passes all understanding.

Attraction

I seek out other sex addicts, and most times I can recognize them. It's weird.

I remember a friend, who was gay, telling me about what he called "gaydar." He was able to recognize people he believed to be gay, and in most cases he was right. Others have told me similar stories.

I know that when I was drinking I was able to determine the drinkers who wanted to drink alcoholically, as I did. It was not purely intuitive—rather, they talked about alcohol in a certain way and always seemed ready to order "another drink."

Sex addicts send their signals to others they believe might be interested. It could involve a certain look, an odd remark, a lingering touch. I suppose "Like attracts like" really is true.

Today I seek out people who are
healthy and in active recovery
for their sex addiction.

Self-Esteem

Is sex addiction the same as love addiction?

Sex addiction and love addiction are not the same, but they can coexist in the same person. Also, the sex addict often is found in a relationship with a love addict.

Let's look at a general definition and explanation of the two addictions:

- *Sex addiction* is compulsive and obsessive behavior concerning sexual activity. Masturbation, porno movies, prostitutes, voyeurism, and Internet chat rooms are often the focus. The driving force definitely revolves around sexual activity, even if it is only to be observed.

- *Love addiction* is more about the need to be in a relationship. It is an aspect of codependency that revolves around the obsession to be in a loving relationship. The love addict is more than willing to give sex in order to feel loved.

Today I seek a loving and sexual
relationship that is based upon mutual respect.
This must include a respect of self.

Generalizations

I think most men, if they are honest,
are sex addicts.

This statement feels more like an excuse for the person to continue sexually obsessive behavior. It conceals an aspect of denial that states, "I'm no different from other men. All men are like me. They are really after one thing: sex!"

This is not true. All drinkers are not alcoholics; all gamblers are not addicts; all men who enjoy a healthy sexual expression in their relationships are not sex addicts.

As a recovering alcoholic, I subscribe to the concept that addiction usually involves a feeling of powerlessness and behaviors that eventually lead to unmanageability. Sex addiction is definitely on the increase in our society, but it is false to say that all men, or all women, are sex addicts.

My spiritual program cautions my
tendency to overgeneralize.

Sharing

*Some sex addicts bequeathed their stories of
recovery before they died. I knew some of them.
They gave me hope. They shared their healing.
They are an important part of my Memorial Day.*

Some people may think that it is a little strange to connect the life and legacy of a sex addict with Memorial Day, but service can be given to the nation in many ways. Surely, helping Americans to remain healthy is an important service. Especially in the early days of the recovery movement, those who courageously and selflessly told what their sex addiction was like, what happened to them, and what changed have provided hope to serve us all.

We all fight many types of war in the service of our fellow men and women. The war that confronts the shame and guilt of sex addiction is not an easy one to wage.

*Thank you for the human gift
of courage that brings hope.*

Spirituality

I don't believe in God. I'm an atheist.
Can I still be spiritual?

Yes, indeed. I know many people who do not believe in God but are extremely spiritual. I have defined spirituality as being a positive and creative human being, and I know people who have walked away from religion who certainly fit this definition.

They are most comfortable with a concept of Higher Power that they describe as an energy that works through nature and, of course, other people.

The foundation of recovery has always been spirituality rather than a particular religion or denomination. The following are seen to be the characteristics of spirituality:

- Willing to surrender our imperfections
- Accepting the need to change
- Seeking an honest program based on service

We call this *a spiritual awakening*.

I believe in a Higher Power that
connects all religions and cultures
and is characterized by love.

Willingness

*Recovery has changed my life. The toughest
decision I made concerning my sex addiction
was asking for help.*

Isn't that the truth! For most people the first step into
recovery is when they are willing to ask for help.

The mix of people who say they are recovering is
interesting because not all of them have received therapy.
Some people have a strong family unit and find that,
once the decision has been made to ask for help, they are
able to maintain abstinence from drugs or alcohol or to
heal from sex addiction. Others find strength in returning to their religious affiliation, discovering a deeper
faith that runs in tandem with their decision to change
their harmful behaviors and negative attitudes. Many
others receive therapy. It is their willingness to see a
therapist or enter into a treatment center for their addiction that enables them to take the first steps to recovery.

*Therapy is an important aspect of my
understanding of spirituality.*

Acceptance

I'm not a religious Jew, but I'm offended when I go to meetings; everyone is talking about Jesus!

I can understand a Jew, a Muslim, a Buddhist, even others, being offended if people at meetings are constantly talking about Jesus or the power of Christianity in their lives. As a recovering alcoholic who has attended 12 Step meetings for many years, I have witnessed some people pushing their love of Jesus or their belief in Christianity. However, in my experience, that happens rarely. Still, it is certainly *not everyone!*

I suggest that when we find a meeting that is not to our liking, we seek out other meetings, other groups. It is not good for anyone in recovery to be attending meetings where they are continually offended. I seek out diverse and nurturing groups to share my recovery from alcoholism.

In my spiritual journey,
I am eager to seek out nurturing
support groups.

Support

My family is supportive. I'm in recovery for my sex addiction. I don't need 12 Step meetings.

It is certainly true that having a supportive family when a person is in recovery from any addiction is helpful. It is also true that many addicts, including sex addicts, who have a supportive family feel that they don't need 12 Step support groups; they heal within the family system.

All this is undeniably true. However, I believe it is important to know that those who have continued recovery and fewer relapses are statistically those who attend 12 Step support groups.

Also, the 12 Step philosophy suggests a spiritual program that is based upon service, unity, and recovery. At the present time it is the best bet for an addict.

> *The three legs that help maintain my recovery are God, Family, and the 12 Step program.*

Self-Hatred

I hate my sexual behavior.

At some point, most addicts hate or despise their behavior. This happens because the progression of the disease creates a negative attitude and destructive behavior patterns, affecting everyone, not least the people that the addict loves.

"I hate my sexual behavior." This statement makes so much sense. However, the question becomes, "What are you going to do about it?"

I've defined spirituality in this book as becoming a positive and creative human being, the opposite of behaving like an addict. This change occurs with help. The sex addict must do something about the behavior he or she detests: go to Sex Addicts Anonymous meetings, seek out a therapist, or go into treatment for an addiction that is creating havoc.

Words must be followed by action. Prayers must be earthed in a change of behavior.

*Today I grasp the things I hate in my life
and create a change in behavior.*

Exploitation

*I raped a girl who was drunk. Actually, I have
raped more than one girl. To have sex, I have
actively searched out girls who were drunk.*

The tragedy of sex addiction, as with alcoholism and
drug addiction, is that it usually involves breaking
the law, as in committing rape. Human beings are used,
in the most despicable ways, to gratify sexual desires.

I remember the young man who told me this in treatment with no obvious remorse; it was more like a report:
"This is what I did. This is where my addiction had
taken me."

But he was in treatment. He was beginning to familiarize himself with the 12 Steps that would require he
seek to make amends, ask for forgiveness, begin the
process of forgiving himself, and then, one day at a time,
seek to carry a message of respect, grounded in the virtue
of peace.

*Great Spirit, I leave behind violence
so that I might experience the
sacred gift of kindness.*

Neediness

My codependency gets me in trouble sexually.
I often will let men have sex with me because
I'm so needy. I hate to be alone.

Although this book specifically addresses sex addiction, an accompanying behavior involves the need to *always* be in a relationship; that is called *love addiction*. The love addict will often speak about the willingness to do anything, even to engage in distasteful aspects of sex, to please the partner and maintain the relationship. The fear is abandonment—being alone.

Love addicts often will attend the same meetings as sex addicts. They get help in creating healthy boundaries, learning to begin to love themselves. Being able to talk about their compulsive need to not be alone, and finding a safe place to express such feelings, is therapeutically helpful. In support groups, they realize that they are not alone.

I am beginning the process of healing by creating
a healthy relationship with myself.

Low Self-Esteem

*I bought a sex enhancer. I've used Viagra,
Levitra, and Cialis—anything. I even seek out
Chinese herbs. And I have no money (sometimes)
for my rent.*

A person often enters therapy or treatment for sex addiction because of financial concerns: The addiction is simply costing too much.

Intervention takes many forms. Financial ruin is common because the stimulants are expensive. Additional costs includes prostitutes, Internet access, and pornographic magazines. Family members are led to the addiction by following the money trail, and then the intervention takes place.

The pain always precedes the cry for help. In the preceding quotation, financial concerns are the motivation, but it doesn't really matter what constitutes the pain as long as the person and family members get the help that is available. Financial ruin can be the catalyst for a miracle.

*Spiritually, I understand that I needed to lose
everything to gain back my life.*

Serenity

Serenity is my goal.

The word *serenity* means "peace." People who are in recovery seek, after many years of negative thinking and destructive behavior, the possibility of moments during which they can *be at one* with themselves, their family, and the world—experiencing, at times, the feeling of peace.

We cannot expect to have serenity every day because challenges that upset our equilibrium will always come along, but we can expect to experience moments when we can feel peace.

The spiritual journey will provide moments when we feel comfortable in our own skin, happy with the life we have, and times when we feel serenity.

Today I enjoy those moments of serenity that come as precious gifts in my recovery.

Remembrance

*I believe I'm healed. Why do I need to say I'm
a sex addict?*

Many people believe, after treatment and a period of
continued recovery, that they are giving power to
the sickness if they say, "I'm a sex addict," that saying so
keeps them in their addiction. The truth is that they
must let go of their old behavior and move on.

As a recovering alcoholic who has been sober many
years, I have some sympathy for this point of view—but
I'm not convinced. When I say, "I'm Leo and I'm an
alcoholic," this statement helps me remember what my
life was like before I embraced recovery. I don't dwell on
the past behavior, but I don't ignore what it was like, and
I believe this thinking helps to keep me sober.

*I remember what it was like to be alcoholic
to better celebrate my recovery.*

Honesty

I was sexually inappropriate at work and was fired. How do I tell my husband?

Sex addiction affects women as well as men. The embarrassment might be greater for women because of the expectations that are placed upon them, but the feelings of powerlessness and unmanageability are the same.

How do you tell loved ones and friends? You tell them within the context of providing information about sex addiction. Perhaps you also get a therapist or psychologist who has experience with sex addiction to join you at this crucial meeting.

A sex addict is not a bad person. Rather, he or she has a compulsive behavior that involves the expression of sexuality. Today, an ever-increasing amount of material covers all aspects of sexual compulsivity. Hopefully the loved one will slowly come to comprehend this addiction. It will not be easy, but honesty will prove to be essential in maintaining a healthy relationship.

Today I demonstrate courage in discussing my sex addiction.

Surrender

In recovery, I'm told to surrender. But I'm a fighter. I never give up.

I remember a friend, who had many years in recovery from alcoholism, telling me that the act of surrender involves the decision to choose life. A person surrenders to live.

Surrender, seen in this light, is not about weakness, but rather it is a conscious choice to let go of behaviors that are causing sadness, despair, and destruction. Surrender involves a different kind of fight—a fight for healing, recovery, and the spiritual life.

It is smart to give up those attitudes and actions that are hurting us. It is smart to know when the fight is lost. It is smart to know when a sickness is destroying a life. Surrender, in recovery, is being smart.

I surrender to live.

Divine Guidance

My recovery from sex addiction—I have four years—has given me divine guidance for my life.

Recovery from any addiction, including sex addiction, is manifested in the spiritual changes we adopt to live our lives. The following are some examples of how some people have maintained recovery:

- Seeking medical and psychological help from a physician or therapist
- Being honest about how they demonstrated sex addiction in their lives
- Having a willingness to consider a spiritual program based upon letting go of some people, places, and behaviors
- Attending support groups and sharing their thoughts, feelings, and actions on a regular basis

The divine guidance is usually experienced by an act of surrender: asking for help.

I have discovered the divine in proportion to my willingness to seek help.

A Dysfunctional Family

I love my father, but he was a sex addict. He arranged my first visit with a prostitute. He encouraged me with serial girlfriends. And I grew to be like my father, except that now I'm at my wits' end.

Parents influence their children. Children often imitate one or both parents, for good or bad. Addictive behavior can be passed down from generation to generation.

In this case, a son enthusiastically seeks to please his father by doing what he requests. For this sex-addicted parent, the rite of passage into manhood involved a visit to a prostitute, then the message that it is a "real man" who can get as many girlfriends as possible, use them, and throw them away. For this son, it resulted in despair.

With the help of a therapist, this son will need to redefine what a healthy man looks like and learn how to treat and respect women.

*I seek to treat all women with
respect and dignity.*

Denial

My wife will not accept that I am a sex addict.
She says I'm exaggerating.

Not only is it very difficult for somebody to accept being a sex addict, but it also is equally difficult for a loved one to accept that the person whom they know intimately is a sex addict. Why? Denial! The very term *sex addict*, more than *alcoholic* or *bulimic*, is fearful and scary for many people, whose minds probably conjure up horrible scenes involving unimaginable sex acts.

Ignorance is always the enemy of good. In the preceding quotation, a possible plan might be to have the wife read more about sex addiction, maybe meet with a therapist who deals with the issues as they relate to the family.

A key recovery theme that is constantly stressed is honesty. Maybe, just maybe, the wife isn't accepting her husband's sex addiction because she doesn't know the full story. Covert and secretive behaviors are the symptoms that often have been used to keep everyone in denial.

If I want people to understand, then
I must be rigorously honest.

Discovery

I hate my sex addiction. It makes me evil.
Why does God allow it?

This quotation touches upon an ancient discussion that philosophers have had with each other for years: Why does God allow evil?

Many philosophers, of all religious persuasions, have suggested that when God bequeathed freedom to humanity, then the *possibility* of evil, of wrongdoing, came into the world.

Sex addicts have a choice: Are they going to continue their unhealthy behaviors, or are they willing to seek help? Recovery is a choice, and recently sex addicts, in great numbers, have been choosing recovery and embarking upon a spiritual journey based upon a conscious decision to change their destructive behaviors and negative attitudes. From a hate of self, the sex addict is discovering a love and respect of self. And, I believe, God is well pleased!

God, in my freedom to choose recovery
rests my spiritual healing.

Suppressed Feelings

Making amends is never easy. I prefer not to say anything. But then I don't experience forgiveness.

Recovery from addiction, especially in the 12 Step program, involves a willingness to make amends. Making amends is the difference between *thinking sorry* and *saying sorry* to another person or persons for what we have said or done.

Can't a person just move into recovery and begin living a different life? It's not that simple. With the disease of addiction, which is often called a "family disease," other people are not only involved but also damaged. The story of Dr. Jekyll and Mr. Hyde, in which two behaviors exist in the same person, is often used as an analogy. When addicts are not "using," they can be loving and gentle, but all hell breaks loose once the drug of choice is taken! Guilt and shame ensue, despair and depression follow, and forgiveness is required. Making amends and delivering an apology usually precede the experience of forgiveness.

*I heal my stubborn pride when
I seek forgiveness.*

Abuse

I've found a drug that makes a person pass out and not remember anything. I mix it with alcohol when a girl comes over to visit. I've even used it with cute boys. It's all about sex.

Date-rape drugs are often used by sex addicts to satisfy their sexual desires. In the 12 Step program, when we say that we have become powerless over our sex addiction and our lives have become unmanageable, we must also understand that we seek to make our victims powerless, creating an unmanageability that is difficult to comprehend.

Women and men become the victims, but the sex addict is also the victim of a tragic life that revolves around being a perpetrator. Love is exchanged for violence, with the possibility of many years in prison.

The healing and recovery will only come with the willingness to receive treatment and begin the long process of behavioral change. Remorse is important, but it is not a substitute for purposeful action.

My healing depends on my willingness to change my behavior.

Responsibility

God made me a sex addict, and I accept it.

I'm sure some religious people would say that God *made you* a sex addict—maybe to test you!

I don't agree.

I don't believe that God creates or "makes" a rapist, racist, sadist, or any addict. I believe that God has given human beings the gift of freedom, and with that gift comes all manner of virtues—and challenges. Unhealthy behaviors and diseases are often passed down from one generation to another; and yes, some of us develop a dependency on alcohol, relationships, and sex.

Why this happens is too complicated a subject for this short meditation, but I do not believe that God "makes" sex addicts nor that God magically "heals" them. We must take responsibility for our challenges. We must get involved in our treatment and recovery. We must do something to create healing.

My responsibility is a powerful aspect of my spirituality.

Sexual Anorexia

*It was hard to admit that I had never been
intimate with anyone. I mean anyone.
My abusive family forced me into isolation.
Now I'm a sexual anorexic.*

The spiritual message I emphasize affirms wellness and recovery. Regardless of the abuse, even in childhood, hope and healing are available.

Most addicts must hear this message, especially sexual compulsives, because of the years of compounded guilt and shame that reinforce the messages: *I cannot change. I will never get well. There is no hope for me.* It is tragic to think how many addicts do not get help, how many die in their addiction, how many commit suicide.

But help and support are available, including for the dysfunctional messages heard in an abusive family. They are available for everyone based on the spiritual belief that human beings are more powerful than *any* addiction, overcoming the morbid feelings of isolation and low self-esteem that feed sexual anorexia.

*Today I live in an attitude
of gratitude.*

Relapse

I had therapy for my sex addiction four years ago. I never attended a support group. Now some old behaviors are returning. What should I do?

"My name is Leo, and I'm an alcoholic." Although I've been sober now for many years, I still introduce myself this way at support meetings. My alcoholism is only one drink away from future alcoholic behavior.

Sex addiction is similar. If we cease to go to meetings and let down our guard against the addictive behavior, it can return in subtle, yet dangerous, ways. The return of some old behaviors is the red flag.

What to do:

- Return to sex addiction recovery meetings
- Go back into therapy
- Seek treatment

Ignoring the warning signs could lead to disaster.

My painful feelings are a gift that prompts me to change my behavior.

Flirting

*From the time I was a young girl, I've been
attracted to men. In recovery I still "weigh up"
men at meetings. Is something wrong with me?*

I do not believe that anything is wrong with a person
being attracted to members of the opposite sex; for
gay men and women, it is natural to find people of their
own sex attractive. But the person in the preceding quotation uses the term *weigh up*, which could indicate that
"stinking thinking" is happening and relapse could be
near.

Sex addicts often sexualize other people, which is
often the precursor to addictive behavior or other aspects
of acting out. I suggest that this person seek out a therapist to discuss what she is doing, or she could discuss the
behavior with her sponsor or share it at a meeting.

*Today I understand that
having unhealthy thoughts is an
opportunity for healing.*

Miracle

*I'm a sexual compulsive, and I'm so ashamed of
my behavior. I went to church looking for magic.
I'm understanding that a miracle is not magic!*

When I'm giving my spiritual lectures I often draw
the distinction between *magic* and *miracle*.

Magic is a trick. In Las Vegas, we might see magicians make animals disappear. I've seen women sawn in
half! But the next night it's the same animal and the
same women in the show. How do they do it? The magicians use lights or mirrors to create an illusion—but it's
not real.

Miracle is real. It requires a change in the individual
addict, an action that can be clearly, visibly demonstrated. The sex addict establishes a personal boundary,
changes behavior, attends therapy and support meetings.
A sex addict must *do something* to experience healing and
recovery.

A helpful saying in recovery meetings is "Pray—but
also move your feet!"

*Great Spirit, I embrace the action
that creates the miracle.*

Questions

Can you be a sex addict and not have problems?

I doubt it. Addiction is, by definition, a lack of balance: a compulsive and obsessive behavior pattern that eventually affects every aspect of our lives.

Addiction is not to be confused with enjoyment. People often repeat what they enjoy. They might occasionally do it to excess, but they invariably get back to balance.

Addiction is manifest when you have *crossed the line*. Most health professionals would say you can never get back. I'm sure some people are able to "catch" themselves and return to a healthy balance without an intervention or recovery program, but most progress into tragically more powerless and unmanageable behaviors.

To end on a positive note, however, I hasten to add that many people are recovering from addiction, including sex addiction, because they are willing to accept that they have a problem.

Spiritually, I realize I am not my problems.
I am able to face and heal
my life's challenges.

Pride

I believe I have the power to recover.
I don't need meetings.

When I visit treatment centers all over the country, I meet patients who share with me that they know they have the power to embrace recovery and they do not need to go to 12 Step meetings. Some achieve exactly what they shared with me in treatment: They stay sober or sexually abstinent, and they do not go to meetings.

However, many relapse. Indeed, in my experience, the vast majority of people who suffer addiction, including sex addiction, relapse soon after ceasing to attend recovery meetings.

The power of the 12 Step program, which involves a spiritual journey, cannot be underestimated in maintaining recovery and healing.

God, I heal my woundedness when I share
with and listen to the wounded.

Spirituality

*I'm Jewish. Most members of Sex Addicts
Anonymous are Christian. The program is not
created for me.*

I can understand a Jewish person feeling awkward in
meetings where the majority of people in the support
group are Christian. However, surely this is a fact of life
for Jewish people living in America: The majority of
people they meet are Christian.

But 12 Step programs are not based on any one religious formula; they are not overtly Christian even
though the majority of members might be Christian.
The 12 Steps are based upon spiritual insights and are
more about a desire to live a positive and creative life
than they are about a religious viewpoint. The 12 Step
program is for everyone: Christian, Jew, agnostic, atheist,
and followers of all other faiths. Humanity in all its
various forms and denominations meets at 12 Step
meetings. The program was created for everyone.

*In 12 Step meetings I celebrate
my shared humanity.*

Honesty

Honesty is a very spiritual ingredient.

When we discuss sex addiction, certain words are used regularly to describe the behavior: *covert, secretive, manipulative, hidden.* The nature of sex addiction necessarily lives in the shadows. Recovery is therefore dependent upon the willingness of the sex addict to be honest, and it is spiritual—not religious.

Spirituality and religion are different in an important way. *Religion* describes a denomination that we are usually born into—for example, Catholics born into a Catholic family, or Muslims born into an Islamic family. *Spirituality* is that divine connection that unites all religious denominations and those who have none. For me, spirituality is about being a positive and creative human being, treating people with the honesty that you would like to receive. In this sense, honesty is often described as the foundation of this spiritual program.

I seek to be honest because
I desire it from others.

Denial

I'm married, but I go to a local park to pick up men. Am I a sex addict?

It is not for me to say who is a sex addict. The key to all addictions are the feelings of remorse, guilt, shame, and utter powerlessness that come from continuing to do the things that create an unmanageable life.

It doesn't really matter if the person asking the preceding question is male or female. We know that dishonesty characterizes the marriage. We also know that the person puts himself or herself at great risk by meeting strangers in a park. We also know that the person has heard about sex addiction: "Am I a sex addict?"

For the sake of the marriage, I suggest that the person see a therapist who specializes in sex addiction and attend a 12 Step support group for sexual compulsivity. In a relatively short time, the person might be able to answer his or her own question.

> *Spiritually, I understand that
> I often ask questions for which
> I already know the answer.*

Toxic Thinking

I'm worried about my behavior around children.
I think crude things when I'm with my
grandchildren. Should I get help?

Sex addiction and sexual compulsivity create inappropriate behaviors that disrespect the boundaries of other people, and this includes children.

Alcoholics often hurt the people whom they love, including children and grandchildren. The mood swings and bouts of violence are uncontrollable, creating what has been called the *dysfunctional home*. Sex addiction, although more covert and secretive by nature, also can invade the boundaries of children and grandchildren. Thoughts can too easily become deeds. Thinking crude things can too easily lead to actual abuse.

Get help now. Begin the necessary conversation with a sex therapist or physician who specializes in treating pedophilia. Explain your crude thoughts in a safe place and know that help is available.

I'm committed to discussing those thoughts
that shame and embarrass me.

Relapse

I was asked to leave a treatment center for alcoholism because I was sexually inappropriate.

Many alcoholics who were treated ten or more years ago were not informed about sex addiction. It simply wasn't talked about. And yet many had *and have* a sex addiction.

Today this situation is a little better. More and more people are learning about sex addiction and sexually compulsive behavior that is the gateway to relapse. Many people, against strict rules at treatment centers that forbid exclusive or sexual liaisons, put themselves at risk of expulsion because they cannot control their sexual behavior. They have a sex addiction, and it will create the same powerlessness and unmanageability as their alcoholism.

Knowledge is power. Today more treatment centers are treating sex addiction simultaneously with alcoholism and drug addiction.

Today I understand I am an obsessive-compulsive. I surrender to treatment in all its manifestations.

Guilt

I spend hours in different restrooms searching for men with whom to have sex. I've been married for twenty years. I'm so ashamed.

Sex addiction creates shame. That toxic shame produces guilt, fear, and low self-esteem. Covert behavior—a life of lies and secrecy—is also involved.

Here we have a married man living a bisexual life in the shadows, and the secret sex is creating shame. How tragic it is to be going from one restroom to another seeking sex from strangers! And yet the euphoria that feeds the sex addiction is probably commingling with the fear, excitement, danger, and suspense that surround this behavior.

Help is available. Many sex addicts have received healing from Sex Addicts Anonymous (SAA) and knowledgeable therapists. The dishonesty must be replaced with self-awareness and self-acceptance.

My first spiritual step began when I was willing to ask for help.

Surrender

*My recovery from sex addiction began with my
understanding of the concept of surrender.*

The 12 Step program, which has been especially helpful for people with alcohol problems, is today used
by people with sex addiction and sexual compulsivity.
The program is essentially spiritual.

With this in mind, we are asked to consider the word
surrender. I see surrender as a willingness to stop a certain behavior that is causing powerlessness and unmanageability. Spiritually, we surrender to live a healthy life.
We surrender to the concept of asking for help, possibly
receiving therapy or treatment. In meetings, we experience the miracle of one sex addict sitting with other sex
addicts, talking about what it was like, what happened,
what life is like now.

Recovery begins when the sex addict is willing not
only to talk about his behavior but also to change it.

*Spiritually, I surrender to
live a healthy life.*

Religious Victimization

I go to church. I believe I'm a faithful Christian. Why is God testing me with my sex addiction?

Some people believe that God is constantly testing them. They say that God never gives us a challenge that we cannot overcome. They take literally the story of Job and say that God sends challenges to assess our faith in Him. This is their answer to earthquakes, famines, and pestilence of all kinds.

I don't hold this view. I don't believe that God is constantly testing us with sickness, violence, and all manner of calamities. Rather, I believe in a world of freedom in which we are personally responsible for what we do or say, personally accountable for how we respond to a particular challenge that comes in our lives. We are not victims unless we choose to be!

The sex addict is free to embrace healing and recovery. Many are doing just that, one day at a time.

Great Spirit, thank you for
the gift of freedom that allows for the
possibility of living a noble life.

Sanity

Did my sex addiction cause me to go insane?

I think the preceding quotation refers to Step Two of the 12 Step program: "Came to believe that a Power greater than ourselves could restore us to sanity." We must be poetic when we consider the past behavior that has led a person to recovery. It would be, for most, too strong a statement to suggest that a person was "insane."

I believe that Step Two is really about living in a fantasy world: not accepting the reality of where sex addiction can take you, its effect upon loved ones, its eventual destruction of all that has been valued or cherished. In this sense, sex addiction can take you into a world of shame, guilt, and fear that is wrapped up in *insane denial.*

Today I choose to live in a world of reality, choosing to see things as they really are.

Freedom

*Independence Day means more to me than
freedom from England's rule. Today I celebrate
my daily reprieve from sex addiction.*

I got sober on the Fourth of July. In 1977, when I first
visited a support meeting for alcoholics, I had no
idea that the Fourth of July was Independence Day in
America. Today, I celebrate my freedom from alcohol
with millions who are celebrating their political freedom.

The preceding quotation celebrates a similar theme:
freedom from the compulsivity that grew around sex.

Can we really compare sex addiction with political
dominance? Yes, in a metaphorical sense, and some
would suggest that sex addiction is *personally* more
painful. Before Independence Day, *all* Americans were
subjects of King George of England, but not everyone is
addicted or a sex addict. Still, the feelings of freedom are
similar: being able to make healthy choices rather than
feeling a slave to obsessive thinking and compulsive reac-
tions. Spirituality always involves a sense of freedom.

*I am spiritually free to show healthy
affection rather than create abuse.*

Unhealthy Behavior

My wife caught me getting the dog sexually excited. She said I was sick. Am I?

You may be "sick" in the sense that you might need therapeutic help.

It is not unusual for sex addicts to use pornography, sex toys, and sadomasochistic experiences to enjoy an ever-greater sexual euphoria—and this occasionally involves animals. Certainly the covert behavior involved in using animals fits the clandestine profile of a sex addict, accompanied by the guilt, shame, and embarrassment of the person involved and his or her family.

Where is the healing? I would suggest that the man in the preceding quotation, and his wife, seek help from a therapist who is skilled in treating sexual compulsivity, in addition to a Sex Addicts Anonymous meeting for the husband and Al-Anon for his wife. Knowing you are not alone is the key to spiritual healing.

*I know my healing depends
upon sharing my secrets.*

Suicide

My sex addiction does not make me feel good. I feel horrible. I've even thought of suicide.

When we hear the preceding words, we see the devastation that can be caused by sex addiction: "I've even thought of suicide."

Addiction is a serious problem in our society. When people think about various addictions that affect people, they don't often consider the epidemic of sex addiction. And yet it is growing at a rapid rate because sex is everywhere, including television, movies, magazines, and the Internet. People say, "It's always been around." That is certainly true, but never has it been marketed and advertised as it has in recent years.

However, recovery from sex addiction is also increasing. People are attending support groups, receiving treatment, entering therapy. People are being saved from suicide.

My spiritual program enables me
to live a creative life.

Identification

I can understand seeing a therapist for my sex addiction, but why do I need meetings with other sexual compulsives?

There is no magic pill for sex addiction. Because sex addiction is "cunning, baffling, and powerful," as Alcoholics Anonymous reminds us, it is important to find support that is available for the rest of our lives, one day at a time.

A therapist who understands sex addiction can play an important and necessary role in the healing of both the addict and the family; however, nobody is expected to stay in therapy for life! People who suffer from addiction, including sex addiction, have been helped by attending self-help support meetings with others who share the same addiction. Hope comes in *seeing* others recovering.

Must you go? No. But those who have studied the recovery process strongly recommend that addicts continue their spiritual journey and healing in support groups.

Today I want to attend recovery support groups.
They are helpful in all areas of
my spiritual growth.

Prayer

I prayed for sexual healing, and it didn't work.
I don't believe in prayer.

I am reminded of a statement attributed to C. S. Lewis: "I do not pray for God alone to hear, but rather that I might hear my prayer."

I suspect that the person quoted prayed, asking God to heal their sex addiction. However, we need also give our prayers feet.

What I mean is that a sex addict, like any other addict, should seek help and support from a therapist, possible treatment, and the ongoing support available in a recovery group such as Sex Addicts Anonymous (SAA).

Prayer is an action word. It requires a person changing his or her attitudes and behaviors to match the words said in prayer.

I pray that I will demonstrate in my life
the aspirations of my prayers.

Respect

Sometimes I like to rub myself in public. A few times strangers have angrily confronted me. I fear I could get arrested.

A healthy society is based upon respect. We do not do things that hurt or disrespect our neighbor. Also we do not expect them to disrespect us.

Sex addiction often can lead, as it does with alcoholism, to public displays of disrespect, illegal behavior, and displays of abuse in a public place.

Recently I read about a Japanese man who was arrested in Tokyo for touching two females inappropriately in the subway. Often men are arrested for public displays of indecency in a toilet.

Sex addicts, if they don't get help, will often drift into illegal behavior and get arrested. Fear is the friend of some addicts. Hopefully, it eventually will lead to seeking help.

Today I affirm that I will not abuse my neighbor.

Questions

What is too much sex?

This is a good question. It is also an appropriate question in a book that addresses sexual compulsivity and sex addiction.

We will be helped to an answer by looking at what is the first step of the 12 Step program that has helped addicts throughout the world.

> We admitted we were powerless over alcohol—that our lives had become unmanageable.

"Too much" is when we are aware of feeling that the sexual behavior is ruling our lives and because of this awareness we are unable to correctly manage our lives.

- Things are getting out of control.
- Loved ones are becoming concerned.
- We feel a devastating shame.

Sex addiction is not about having an active sex life but a dysfunctional one.

*Spiritually, I know I need balance
in my sexual expression.*

Isolation

*My sex addiction separated me from my
spiritual family.*

Any addiction will eventually separate a person from
his or her spiritual family because addiction, by its
very nature, is unbalanced, negative, and eventually
destructive.

If you have a sex addiction, then by definition you
are consumed, obsessed, and compulsive around aspects
of sexuality. Each sex addict would have his or her own
particular peccadillo, but it would eventually destroy his
or her spiritual life.

What do you do when you know this is happening?
You begin to get back on track. Confront what your
sexual behavior is and seek the necessary help. What
would be unconscionable would involve denying the
addictive behavior, hoping it might heal itself or simply
get better without a concerted effort to change.

*Today I know that my spiritual journey is
essential to my long-term happiness.*

Arrogance

Recovery is for wimps!

I've heard many people say just this in myriad forms. Some were addicts who were in denial. Some did not have an addiction issue and had no empathy for compulsive people. Some said the statement was funny!

The truth is that anybody who faces an addiction and seeks recovery is showing great courage. It is particularly difficult for a sex addict to be honest before family and friends, so an addict enters treatment and begins discussing shaming issues with a therapist or attends Sex Addicts Anonymous meetings and shares with fellow addicts who are, initially, strangers.

People who know a recovering addict usually describe the addict's transformation as "courageous." Recovery is definitely *not* for wimps!

My recovery demonstrates
God's courage in my life.

Shame

*I feel so ashamed of my sex addiction. I'm a
mother of three children and have a great
husband, but I seek out men when I go shopping,
especially in supermarkets. I've had sex with
them when the children were in the house!*

I remember hearing these words from a patient and
thinking that if I passed her in the street I would
never think that she was a sex addict. She looked like
most women I see shopping in supermarkets.

Such an attitude reflected my ignorance. What does
a sex addict look like? What does an alcoholic or gam-
bler look like? Like you and me.

Even though I missed it, the woman's despair was
apparent. She hated what she had become. Shame, without added adjectives, cannot describe how she felt. The
pain almost drove her to suicide.

Yet she had made it into treatment and was doing
well. She was learning about her addiction and how to
establish boundaries and maintain an active recovery.

*It is often the pain we experience in life that
pushes us toward change and healing.*

Surrender

I hear people say that it's hard to heal from sex addiction. I disagree. The pain I experience in recovery is nothing like the guilt and shame I created for myself as a sex addict.

It is important to choose our words carefully. Also, we must make sure that what we are saying is not simply something that we are repeating. What we say must resonate with how we actually feel.

If we give energy to constantly repeating how difficult it is to get recovery, then we become self-defeating. Plus, in most cases it is not true that recovery is difficult. Therapy and treatment make healing a challenge, but in no way does that compare with the situations created by an active addiction: the shame, remorse, legal issues, divorce, and possible incarceration.

In recovery, my worst day is better than my best day as an addict.

Seeking Help

*This is the second job I have lost due to my
inappropriate sexual behavior with the
office staff.*

The sexually inappropriate behavior of the sex addict
is sometimes taken into the workplace. We should
not be surprised. Although addicts try to keep their
addiction confined to days off or evenings only, in most
cases the addiction cannot be controlled. That's what
makes it an addiction!

As in the story of Dr. Jekyll and Mr. Hyde, which is
often seen as a template for addictive behavior, Mr. Hyde
eventually takes over Dr. Jekyll—killing him.

More misfortune will await the sex addict until he or
she begins a program of recovery, possibly seeking therapy
and treatment. It is not enough to recount the tragedies
and pray for change. The addict must embark upon a
course of behavioral change that leads to healing.

*I am ready to seek help for
my sexually addictive behavior.*

Prejudice

I only date Mexican women. I enjoy humiliating them sexually. I'm also a recovering alcoholic.

Some heterosexuals seem to hate women. They enjoy hurting them, making them suffer. Often this is unconscious, but it is clear that their behavior toward men is different from how they treat women.

This is more than sexism. This is abuse. If we add racism to this behavior, then we can see how certain populations, or cultures, are sought out and then cruelly ridiculed, often violently.

Therapy will explore the source of this behavior. In our brokenness, we can lash out so easily at others. Racism is still an issue in our society, and when it gets twisted with a sex addiction, humiliation becomes commonplace. Notice that the preceding quotation doesn't infer any remorse.

An understanding of an inclusive and respectful spirituality and some extensive therapy are essential for this person's healing and recovery.

I am willing to share my darkest secrets in order to heal.

Pornography

I'm watching pornography almost every night. I'm starting to get worried about my behavior because I occasionally watch it at work.

We know we have a problem when it starts to get out of control: the drug addict who seeks drugs from strangers on the streets, the alcoholic who drives to work intoxicated from the previous evening's binge, the compulsive eater who lies about the amounts eaten—and yes, the sex addict who looks at pornography on the computer at work.

The unhealthy behavior progresses, it escalates, the powerlessness becomes obvious.

It is good to worry. "No gain without pain." Hopefully, the anxiety will lead to support, possible treatment, and therapy.

Tragedy usually strikes those with an addictive nature who don't worry.

Thank you, Great Spirit, that
I have worry in my life.

Unmanageable

*I go to a gay bar to pick up men. I feel I must
have sex with someone; otherwise I have failed.
If it gets late, I'll have sex with anyone.*

When I see the word *desperate*, I often must place it
in the context of a story or an incident. The preceding quotation tells me how desperate a person can
get for affection and companionship.

Here we experience the loneliness of the sex addict.
Some may feel he is more a romance or love addict; certainly he is lonely, desperate, suffering low self-esteem.
As an alcoholic, I can identify with the feelings; my pickup was alcohol.

My understanding of spirituality involves love of self,
which is often the healing balm for that codependent
and needy behavior that leads us to seek the company of
anyone rather than be alone.

Spirituality tells us that we are enough.

*I'm seeking to develop a healthy
relationship with myself.*

Seeking Help

I've been inappropriate with both my daughters.
What should I do?

Sex addiction does not have boundaries, and many addicts realize that they have been inappropriate in many areas of their lives, including with family members.

What should a person who has been inappropriate with children do? See a therapist. Speak honestly with a psychiatrist who understands sex addiction. Depending on what has occurred, a report may need to be submitted to the local health authorities, and legal issues could ensue. There are often serious consequences to sexually addictive behavior, certainly if it concerns minors.

Whatever the consequences, the person concerned should be willing to embark upon a course of treatment that will provide healing and a spiritual understanding of forgiveness and recovery.

Spiritually, I understand
and accept my responsibility for
inappropriate behavior.

Therapy

I go to 12 Step meetings, but I'm still sexually promiscuous.

If the individual is not going to Sex Addicts Anonymous (SAA), then he or she should do so; the promiscuous behavior may cease. However, if the person is going to SAA and is still promiscuous, then therapy and treatment may be required.

It is important to remember that a 12 Step program is not therapy. Rather it is a group of people who have the same addiction, meeting together to share, listen, and grow on a daily basis. No counseling is provided. Issues of abuse, dysfunctional families, or traumas are mentioned in a most general way. It is undeniable that some sex addicts need more than a support group.

*My spiritual program requires
that I seek the help I need.*

Balance

*12 Step programs push religion. They insist
I believe in God.*

It is not true that 12 Step programs push religion.
Neither is it true that they insist you believe in God.
It *is* true that some members of this fellowship are
overzealous in their efforts to bring a person to God, or
a religion, or a church. However, this is not the 12 Step
fellowship—it is individuals, and it is unfortunate.

If we read the "official" writings that are put out by
the 12 Step fellowship, we will see that they are *very* sen-
sitive about distinguishing spirituality from religion.
Indeed, the writings often use the term *Higher Power*,
and when they do refer to God, they add "as you understand Him." This gives us a great deal of freedom.

It is true that some addicts, after entering recovery,
return to the religion or church of their childhood—but
they do so with a different attitude. Such people are able
to marry a spiritual philosophy with organized religion.

*I believe in a God who works through
the religious and the nonreligious,
creating love and acceptance.*

Reality

I'm a sex addict and, honestly, I'm still attracted to women. Have I relapsed?

Recovery from sex addiction does not mean that we do not continue to find the opposite sex attractive or beautiful. In a similar way, the homosexual will continue to find people of the same sex equally attractive and beautiful.

However, our thoughts can be a warning signal that all is not well with our recovery program. We have not relapsed, *but danger is present*. We can address this by talking with our sponsor, or—if we feel safe in doing so—by sharing at a meeting. There's a fine line between finding people attractive and sexualizing them. Honesty is the key to continued healing.

I understand that my thinking
is the doorway to recovery
and possible relapse.

Shame

Why does talking about my sex addiction cause me to feel so ashamed?

Few people feel comfortable talking about *anything* that is sexual. Sex, for most people, is the pink elephant that lives in the house while people walk around it!

Religion has tended to condemn any sexual behavior outside of marriage. Society, influenced by religion, has suggested that respectable people do not discuss sex in polite conversation. Thus, all things sexual have become taboo topics.

Is this changing? Yes. Younger people, in all societies, have a more open attitude about sex and are able to discuss it honestly. However, this has probably been happening only in the last twenty years. Still, a residual guilt and shame persist.

In my experience, anyone who feels shame about their sex addiction should seek help from a therapist or attend a sex addiction support group.

*I am willing to find a safe arena
to discuss my sex addiction.*

Religious Abuse

My husband wants sex too often. He hurts me sometimes. When I complain, he says it is my duty as a wife.

The inference here is what I call "religious abuse": "It is my duty as a wife." Occasionally, fundamentalist Christians will suggest, based on Scripture that suggests a wife *must* obey her husband, that a spouse *must* perform sexual behaviors even if they make her uncomfortable. Those religious fanatics who are also sex addicts would certainly manipulate Scripture to gain sexual favors.

No healthy husband would wish to knowingly hurt his wife. No healthy husband would wish to have sex with his wife if she felt uncomfortable or unwilling. Remember: Sex addicts are not healthy.

Healing can only come into this relationship if the wife is willing to get help and arrange an intervention on her husband. Does this happen? Yes. And treatment and recovery are available.

*Today I understand that I am a
child of God, not a slave.*

Ignorance

My sponsor for my alcoholism says I don't need to go to Sex Addicts Anonymous meetings.

An AA sponsor may be a fine person and knowledgeable about alcoholism. However, he or she may not be qualified to be a 12 Step sponsor for any other addiction. Indeed, an AA sponsor may know little about the symptoms of sex addiction or the dynamics of an eating disorder and so on.

Sex addiction has become rampant in our society because of a mixture of ignorance, denial, and hypocrisy. Sex, at best, is a difficult subject to talk about seriously; it tends to be wrapped in humor and innuendo. The Alcoholics Anonymous community is not immune to this. Indeed, I'm convinced that many recovering alcoholics, both men and women, are untreated sex addicts.

Better to seek advice and therapy from a health professional who understands the symptoms and the treatment programs available for sexual healing.

Today I understand that I need not always follow the advice that I am given.

Love Addiction

*I'm crazy for romance. It has caused me major
problems and heartache. But sex I can take
or leave.*

A recovery program that is closely connected with
Sex Addicts Anonymous (SAA) is Sex and Love
Addicts Anonymous (SLAA). Of course, it is possible
to be both a sex addict and a love addict, but for most
love addicts sex is not the focus. The obsession is for
romance: to be loved, to feel cared for in a relationship
with someone (almost anyone!). And, yes, in many cases,
the love addict would be prepared to exchange sex for
feeling loved.

Love addiction is related to low self-esteem, probable
shame issues, and a lack of spirituality that would manifest itself in low self-worth and unhealthy boundaries.

Al-Anon and other codependency programs already
exist to help the love addict, but it can be good to experience S-Anon for families and friends of the sex addict.

*I am never truly alone when I can
love and respect myself.*

Voyeurism

*For years I've placed a hidden camera in my
bathroom. Later I watch what took place.
Needless to say, I have hours of tape.*

The unmanageability of sex addiction often involves a most natural aspect of life: time. The addict squanders time doing the following:

- Watching videotapes for hours, waiting for a sexually euphoric moment
- Spending hours on the Internet
- Waiting alone in a damp public bathroom for a stranger to enter
- Driving for hours at night while looking for someone to indicate an interest

Add to such activities the worry about being caught, the fear of being found out, and the embarrassment of having one's name published in a newspaper. For some addicts, this fear and anxiety seem to add to the euphoria, and danger becomes strangely attractive.

*Today I have made the decision to get
help for my clandestine behavior.*

Fear

*I'm a mother of two children. I'm ashamed of my
sex addiction. I think if I tell a therapist that
my children will be taken away.*

We know that shame creates fear: "What will people
think about me?" In the preceding quote, a
mother expresses the fear of losing her children. This
fear is real. Depending on the severity of the sex addiction and the behavior associated with it, social services
might need to get involved.

In any case, doing nothing is not the answer. As for
any sickness, the sooner treatment and help are requested,
the sooner the healing begins.

Today, help for sex addiction is available, and people
are recovering. Support groups exist in every state and
most cities. Education and understanding are growing
rapidly, and the result is healing. With this healing comes
the feeling of safety.

*My spiritual healing is being
extended to members of my family
and close friendships.*

Surrender

*I'm willing to embrace a spiritual program, but
I don't want to make any amends.*

The word *surrender* is purposefully used in relationship to spirituality because it suggests having
reached a point in the battle with addiction where the
addict is willing to do *anything* to get his or her life
back. Progress cannot be made in any recovery program
if conditions are set, so one must surrender to the belief
that Higher Power or other people know how to stop
the addiction, even when the addict doesn't. As 12 Step
people often say, "You are willing to get out of your
own way."

Making amends is simply a matter of saying "Sorry"
to the people who have been hurt because of an addiction. Making amends enables the addict to let go of the
burden of past abuses so that he or she can embark upon
a spiritual journey based upon kindness and respect.

Why should a person who wants recovery object to
making amends?

*I make amends so I can embrace
spiritual freedom.*

Optimistic

I go to sex addiction recovery meetings often.
I have a sponsor. My life is slowly getting
on track.

Sex addicts are getting better. Recovery and sexual healing happen daily.

Why should we be surprised? Millions of alcoholics, drug addicts, food addicts, and others suffering from compulsive behaviors are getting recovery in 12 Step programs. Why wouldn't sex addicts experience the same?

The challenge is to begin the conversation that allows people to discuss sex addictions and the shamed behaviors that are involved. It is the secrecy that stops recovery; it is the secrecy that kills.

Hello. My name is _____,
and I am a sex addict.

Questions

Is sex addiction hereditary?

This is a most interesting question. From what I understand from the professionals who have studied and worked with sex addicts, the consensus is "No." However, we are all influenced by the people among whom we grow up, especially family. As we know, many sex addicts have picked up attitudes and behaviors from a father, mother, or sibling.

People are incredibly imitative. We copy the voice, walk, dress, and sexual attitudes of the people around us. When Michael Jackson first grabbed his crotch on stage, it wasn't long before rappers and others imitated his behavior.

Sex addiction may not be hereditary, but it can certainly be fostered and nurtured by family and associates. That is why it is important to stress the spiritual insight that human beings are capable of powerful changes and decisions. We can all choose wellness.

Today I understand that I am born into
a family but am also an individual.

August

Obsessive

I really enjoy sex. I think about it all the time.
Does that make me a sex addict?

You are not a sex addict just because you enjoy sex. However, if you think about it all the time, you might have a problem.

People often exaggerate when they talk about sex, particularly their sexual prowess or adventures. The preceding quotation may contain such an exaggeration.

When we seek to define sex addiction, we are helped by information gained over many years concerning other addictions. A key phrase springs to mind: "feelings of powerlessness and unmanageable behaviors." The sex addict invariably experiences a lack of balance concerning sexual expression, with sexual behaviors becoming worrisome. Surely an obsessive thinking pattern concerning sex is a symptom of addiction.

Spiritually, I enjoy sex—alongside many
other pleasures that life provides.

Serenity

*What does recovery from sex addiction mean
to me? Well, my marriage survived the despair.
My children are proud of me. And I have
self-respect.*

When we discuss sex addiction, we can so easily get
stuck in the shame and despair that inevitably
characterize the illness. People's lives are destroyed,
spouses are manipulated, children are abandoned, police
and the courts get involved, and relationships are ruined.

But this is only part of the story. We must not forget
about treatment and recovery. In the preceding quotation, a *spiritual awakening* has healed an unhealthy marriage; the children involved have accepted their parents'
sex addiction and are proud of the ongoing recovery; and
the sex addict has found self-respect.

Say yes to your sexual healing. Thousands are receiving
help.

> *The healing of my sex addiction
> has brought me into a deeper
> relationship with my family.*

Insanity

I got caught having sex on an airplane with a girl I didn't know. They let us both go without making a report.

Most of us have read accounts of crazy and insane behaviors related to drug abuse and alcoholism. Sex addiction reveals a similar insanity—with potentially major legal consequences.

The key to healing and recovery must begin with an acceptance of the basic belief that the energy that surrounds sex can become addictive. Few would dispute this when they consider the ever-increasing presence of pornography on the Internet and in magazines and advertising, as well as the rampant increases in the human sex trade and sex crimes involving adults and children.

Therapy, treatment, and ongoing support are essential for healing, depending on the severity of an individual's sex addiction. A spiritual approach that moves the individual from shame and sin, focusing on acceptance and the possibilities of changes in behavior, is also necessary.

Today I live an honest, spiritual program that affirms healing one day at a time.

Worry

I can't stop worrying about my sex addiction.

Some things we *must* worry about. Sex addiction is certainly not something to blow off as being unimportant. Indeed, it can and has destroyed lives.

However, worrying is a little like prayer: It is important to experience, but at some point it must be translated into action. Otherwise, in the words of a famous saying, we can "worry ourselves to death."

I've always felt that spirituality is a choice we make to express a positive and creative life. Spirituality utilizes meditation and prayer to change attitudes and behaviors. In this sense, it is extremely practical.

Spirituality asks these questions:

- Are we willing to confront the addiction and get help?
- What are we going to change?
- What are we willing to do?

Only when we are willing to answer these questions can we move into recovery.

*Lord, I believe I am willing and able to
change my destructive behaviors.*

Information

Is sex addiction a new sickness? It's only in recent years that people are talking about it.

Sex addiction hasn't been talked about until relatively recently, as it has surfaced in the recovery community over the previous twenty years. Thanks to the pioneering work of Dr. Patrick Carnes, many alcoholics and drug addicts are recognizing their compulsivity regarding their sexual behavior. Indeed, many relapses have been traced back to sexual triggers that eventually led back to the addict's drug of choice.

Today most treatment centers and therapists have a superficial knowledge of sexually compulsive behaviors, and Sex Addicts Anonymous (SAA), Sexaholics Anonymous (SA), Sex and Love Addicts Anonymous (SLAA), and Co-dependents of Sex Addicts (COSA) have become fast-growing support groups.

Knowledge is power. When people discuss the behavior and symptoms of sex addiction, it opens the door to healing and recovery.

My spiritual program teaches me to speak out honestly about sex addiction issues.

Secrets

I'm a lesbian, but I'm married to a man. I secretly have sex with some of my girlfriends.

Secrecy and covert behavior are the key ingredients of sex addiction. Alongside this deception, we also often encounter manipulation, dishonesty, and a tragic loneliness created by living in the shadows.

From the preceding quotation, I cannot determine if the wife is a sex addict, but I certainly sense that she is spiritually wounded because she is living a lie. She is blocking a possible loving relationship with another woman. She is using her girlfriends and her husband. And the secrets support the denial.

Spirituality requires honesty. Spirituality proclaims the dignity of self-disclosure. Spirituality affirms risks that take us out of the shadows.

Today I am proud of all my intimate relationships.

Spirituality

I am Jewish. I had always thought that the 12 Step program was Christian. However, in SAA I meet Jews, Hindus, Muslims, atheists, agnostics, and others. It's a Fellowship, not a denomination!

The 12 Step program is based upon a tried-and-true formula for changing lives. It is available in almost every country in the world. Every type of human being and religious believer attends.

I define *spirituality* as a human being positive and creative. The spiritual teachings that are involved in the 12 Step program are suggestions only. In its concern to treat the family, the program offers support for friends and family members, promising the same spiritual awakening.

Each person will have a different experience, but for me the spiritual awakening involved a respect for self.

*My spiritual program is based upon
a respect for myself and others.*

Covert Behavior

*For ten years I've been in recovery for drug
addiction. I tell everyone I'm in recovery, but
I keep my sexual compulsivity a secret.*

"We are only as sick as our secrets" has become a
popular saying in therapy, particularly as it
applies to addiction.

With sex addiction, the guilt and shame issues are
compounded by society's inability to talk meaningfully
about sex. People joke about sex, snigger at sex, and
exaggerate sexual performance; rarely is the subject faced
seriously and honestly. Religion has played a significant
role in fostering this secrecy: Dogma dictates that sex,
other than in heterosexual marriage, was, and still is, a
really *bad* sin.

Most sex addicts are in the closet. Many recovering
addicts find it difficult to talk about their sexually compulsive issues. Dishonesty and possible relapse result
when this addiction goes unaddressed. That is tragic!

*My spiritual program insists
that I embrace reality.*

Voyeurism

I've become a Peeping Tom. I enjoy using binoculars to stare into windows from my apartment.

Sex addiction takes you into some really strange areas. The term *Peeping Tom* has been around for years, and now we are able to consider this behavior in terms of a sex addiction.

Imagine being a wife or lover of someone who spends his evenings staring into other people's homes. Can you imagine the shame and embarrassments? And, if Peeping Tom wants to hide his behavior, then he must indulge in tremendous covert maneuverings that will eventually affect everyone he loves—not to mention the stress felt by him due to the fear of being caught.

Intervention would be required for a Peeping Tom. Family and friends might be the best ones to deliver the message: "Enough is enough."

I affirm that intervention is often a necessary ingredient for spiritual healing.

Low Self-Esteem

My penis is too small. I love to see big ones.
That's really why I joined the gym.

Sex addicts often obsess generally about all aspects of sexuality. Others focus their obsession on a particular object.

Sex addiction thrives in secrecy, guilt, shame issues, abuse, low self-esteem, and occasionally self-hatred. The man quoted here feels "less than" because his penis is too small. His seeing "big ones" can only reinforce his already established self-loathing. Thus, attending the gym feeds the sick cycle that revolves around euphoria ("I love to see big ones") and self-hatred ("My penis is too small").

A Sex Addicts Anonymous (SAA) meeting would be helpful in such a situation. The sex addict could certainly find guidance from a sponsor in SAA, and therapy could be transformative.

My spiritual goal is self-acceptance.
I must heal. I must seek help.

Shame

*I've told some friends that I'm a sex addict, but
I will never tell people I have AIDS. I'm enjoying
my life one day at a time.*

A certain selfishness permeates addicts who are not willing to be completely honest. This is certainly true for those suffering from a sex addiction.

I can understand a person not wanting to share that he or she has AIDS, but it becomes worrisome when I hear, "I will never tell people that I have AIDS." Saying "never" rules out any possibility of change or growth. Also, some people have a right to know, especially a sexual partner.

What is also confusing in this quote is the statement "I'm enjoying my life one day at a time." This tends to imply a recovery philosophy. However, one person's enjoyment could create a disaster for others. Spiritually speaking, our enjoyment should never be at the expense of others.

*I am learning, in my daily recovery,
never to say never!*

Common Sense

I can give up alcohol and smoking. How do you give up sex?

Who said you must give up sex? Only in extremely rare cases is abstinence the suggested therapy for the sex addict. Recovery involves living *with* our sexuality—not running away from it.

In this sense it might be helpful to compare the sex addict with a person suffering from an eating disorder: He or she is not expected to cease eating! Rather, a therapeutic technique I'm familiar with suggests we make friends with food and seek, spiritually, to create a balance in an eating plan. In a similar way, it is the negative attitudes and destructive behaviors that create the sex addiction that must be addressed therapeutically so that a balanced recovery plan can be applied in daily life.

Sex is a spiritual gift from God. Never should it be condemned as evil. As with anything, it can be abused—but its essential *goodness* remains.

I work in my recovery to create balance
and respect in the expression
of my sexuality.

Balance

*My boyfriend and I are sex addicts. It's a great
relationship. We both know what we want and
what we like.*

I don't know many people who would think that being
a sex addict, in a relationship with another sex addict,
was the basis for a "great relationship."

Maybe we are quibbling about terminology. Perhaps
the person means that she and her partner enjoy sex,
have their needs met, and have sex with regularity. But
that is not sex addiction.

Sex addiction is about an all-consuming thinking or
behavior concerning sex that, like any other addiction,
creates havoc. Balance and boundaries are absent. And it
eventually creates unmanageability.

Addiction is a negative for any relationship.

*Spiritually, I understand the difference
between enjoying sex and
being a sex addict.*

Openness

Treatment is hard for me. Years ago I faced my alcoholism, but I find it difficult to talk about my sexual exploits. It's too shameful.

Treatment is difficult. Recovery from alcoholism is not easy. Certainly we know that tremendous shame is associated with sex addiction. However, is that a reason for not doing anything?

We often hear an internal message that we constantly repeat to others, eventually believing it. However, occasionally this message is only partially true.

At first we affirm and believe that it is harder to remain abstinent than it is to recover. It can be shaming to talk about a sex addiction, but it can be more shaming to ignore or deny it. We must change the negative messages in our heads that continue to keep us stuck. When we embrace the concept of spirituality—being positive and creative—the ways we think of and discuss addiction change.

I'm open to confronting my shame in order to embrace healing and recovery.

Courage

I'm fourteen. My stepfather touches me
inappropriately when Mom is not around.
What can I do?

Sex addiction often leads to inappropriate and illegal behavior, which can be criminal in nature. Children and teenagers are all too often sought and used to satiate sexual urges. The preceding quotation points out sexual abuse.

It is sad that this teenager is not able to talk with his or her mother. It is tragic to feel so isolated. However, the teenager is asking for help.

I suggest reporting the abuse to a family member, clergy, or school counselor. Once the report has been filed, the healing can begin—for everyone.

The stepfather is not a bad person, but he *is* sick and unhealthy. Everyone in this family needs therapeutic help. Healing begins when the secrets are exposed.

Spiritually, I understand that victims are
not guilty but need help and healing.

Abuse

My therapist encourages me to have sex with him. He says it will help me in developing intimate relationships.

It is a cliché to suggest that nobody is perfect, but it's true, including therapists. We have corrupt officers of the law, politicians, teachers, physicians, clergy—and yes, therapists. It is a fact we must come to terms with and accept. Corruption and manipulation by people in power are here to stay.

Compulsive sex takes us into danger zones and breaks down healthy boundaries, so a patient and healer should never commingle. Relationships with clients are always inappropriate. Regardless of what a therapist might say, he or she should *never* be intimate with a patient. If that tenet is violated, the therapist must be reported.

The pain and shame experienced in these danger zones might prompt the intervention that is the key to treatment and healing. The professional pain of being reported and placed on probation could provide the necessary intervention that would provide treatment and recovery.

Today I refuse to give away my power.

Education

*What is the difference between treatment
and recovery?*

Treatment and recovery are closely associated, but
with a difference.

Treatment is when we seek out a therapist or treatment center to specifically address the behavior that is
causing distress and health problems in our life. The
length of treatment varies, but the therapy is invariably
focused upon major behavioral changes.

Recovery, in the context of addiction, is the willingness to surrender to one or more support programs in
which people with a problem help others, which is
euphemistically referred to as *self-help*.

For those suffering from sex addictions, the main
support groups are Sex Addicts Anonymous (SAA),
Sexaholics Anonymous (SA), Sex and Love Addicts
Anonymous (SLAA), and Sexual Compulsives Anonymous (SCA).

*Today I am open, if necessary, to treatment
and ongoing spiritual support.*

Honesty

I've been dating a girl for six months. I really like her. Should I tell her I'm a sex addict?

Sex addiction is not an easy topic to talk about. At the time of writing, my sister is visiting me from England, and it wasn't easy to discuss this book with her. For most people, a peculiar shame pervades the topic of sex, so that it's not a subject for polite conversation.

With this as background, I'm able to sympathize with the preceding question: "Should I tell her I'm a sex addict?"

Personally I think that sex addiction must be discussed; otherwise it will stay forever immersed in covert behavior and secrecy. I've discussed my alcoholism with good friends, and I hope that sex addicts are able to do the same.

The spiritual life is often experienced when a person makes the tough decision to move toward rigorous honesty, because "the truth will set you free."

*In my developing relationship with God,
I seek to be honest in all my affairs.*

Support

I attend a church searching for help for my sex addiction. It isn't helping.

Without wishing to discount any church or religious institution, houses of worship may not be the first place for the sex addict to go for help. Addiction is a mental health challenge. It involves behavioral health. Indeed, therapy might require confronting some unhealthy religious messages that we heard during our childhood or teenage years, such as these:

- Sex is only for making children.
- Masturbation is a horrid sin.
- Gay people who do not repent are destined for Hell.

Sex Addicts Anonymous (SAA), which can be found in most cities, and any addictions treatment center would be able to provide contact information.

After we have experienced professional help, our attendance and involvement with a church might prove to be spiritually refreshing and helpful. First things first!

God's healing power is demonstrated through caring and informed professionals.

Irresponsibility

I'm ashamed to say that I was completely
irresponsible in my sex addiction. I'm
HIV-positive, but I had unprotected sex.
Sex really did consume me.

It is good to read that this person is willing to confront this irresponsible behavior. Having unprotected sex and knowing you are HIV-positive reveals a certain callousness and disrespect toward the people with whom we are intimate.

However, spirituality is always about forgiveness. It is comforting to believe that God has forgiven us, but it is also important to forgive ourselves. It is never a good thing, in recovery, to be constantly beating ourselves up about past behaviors.

I notice that the preceding quote ends in the past tense: "Sex really did consume me." We hope that this person is active in recovery, establishing healthy boundaries and engaging in a positive and creative life.

Today I am able to forgive
my past behaviors.

Impotence

I'm impotent, but I'm still sex crazy.

The sex addict is not necessarily involved in physical sex. He or she can be the voyeur, the listener on the phone, and even the impotent. Sex addiction is centered on the euphoria experienced through the brain, on feeling excited.

I do not want to suggest you are a sex addict if you enjoy pornography, just as I would not say that a person who occasionally gets drunk is alcoholic. Yet how we describe and express our sexual behavior often provides insight as to what is really going on—in this case, the quotation says, ". . . but I'm still sex crazy." That is the addict's words!

I sense in the preceding quotation a loneliness and shame that are unspoken.

The spiritual answer is a healthy relationship in which love can be expressed and experienced. It need not be sexual, and it certainly isn't crazy.

Today I am able to love and
respect who I am.

Love

In recovery I've discovered that sex is not love.

I cannot tell you how many times I've heard clients receiving treatment for an addiction make the preceding statement. Indeed, although I was raised in the church, as a recovering alcoholic I thought that sex and love were connected, if not the same!

Recovery teaches us that love and sex are not the same. Indeed, some of the most loving relationships we might experience in our lives are not sexual. Love can be derived from family and friends, the camaraderie felt in recovery meetings, the experience of enjoying a love related to God or a Higher Power. Love need not involve sex, and often sex does not involve love.

We need always remember that sex is a precious gift from God and that sexual love is *not* less than other forms of loving expressions, although all manifestations of love are not necessarily interchangeable.

Today I am able to understand and
respect a love that is not sexual.

Denial

*I know sex addicts who are happy. Why am
I so fearful?*

Few using addicts, if any, are happy, because addiction is never a healthy or positive behavior. It is a negative.

Enjoying work is different from having a work addiction.

Being a gourmand is not the same as being a compulsive eater.

Having a satisfied and fully expressed sexual life is hardly the same as being a sex addict.

Addiction does not make people feel happy.

The spiritual program that has been developed in addressing addiction stresses the need for balance, respect, and healthy boundaries. It is these spiritual behaviors that create happiness.

*My spiritual program is slowly
creating a personal happiness based upon
respect for myself and others.*

Surrender

I was reported for being sexually inappropriate with a coworker, but I could not stop myself. I need help.

I've been a spiritual advisor for addiction programs for many years, and I'm familiar with words such as *addiction, obsession, compulsion,* and *fanaticism* for the religious addict. For most people, the feelings of unmanageability and powerlessness create fearful chaos: "But I could not stop myself." That says it all for the sex addict who feels unable to control the inappropriate behavior!

In the preceding quotation, fortunately we hear surrender: "I need help." That is the door to healing. Yes, prayers and going to church will help, and reading the Bible firms up this intention—*but change comes with action.*

Spirituality offers a practical philosophy based upon getting our healthy needs met: seeing the therapist, and attending Sex Addicts Anonymous (SAA) and other support groups to do the necessary footwork.

My prayer is simple:
I'm ready to do what it takes.

Masturbation

My husband masturbates too much. He says only three times a day, but I know it's more. How can I help him?

Compulsive masturbation is a common behavior of many sex addicts. Because of prior religious teachings concerning the sinfulness of masturbation, it is a rarely discussed topic. Secrecy and covert behavior, often created by rigid religious teachings, surround the discussion of sex addiction, which surely includes masturbation.

I believe that help will come to families when they seek therapy from a mental health professional experienced in treating sex addiction. It is said that "we are only as sick as our secrets." The dishonesty referenced in the preceding quotation is probably based upon the husband's profound guilt and shame. He is in denial. Therapy will help the husband and the wife journey to a spiritual program based upon honesty.

I will seek to spiritually understand the roots of my shame.

Dishonesty

*I'm dishonest in every relationship. I'm always
unfaithful, but I get jealous if my girlfriend looks
at another man.*

Jealousy is not logical. Often we hate to see in another
that which we know about ourselves. Judgments and
anger invariably reflect our own insecurities. We do not
like our personal shame to be reflected in the actions of
another.

We have associated words for this behavior: *controlling, insecure, shallow*—the list goes on. However, what
we really see is shame: an acute insecurity, a profound
dislike of who we really are and an inability to face it.

Recovery will reinforce self-forgiveness. Spirituality
will affirm self-esteem. Healing will produce acceptance.

*Today I am on the journey toward
self-acceptance and self-love.*

Confusion

*My religion forbids sexual intercourse before
marriage. That was the real reason I married
Jack. It was never for love—it was for sex.*

Whatever the religious teachings intended, they have
been twisted and manipulated. Rigid religious
morality has become connected to covert, secretive sexual
behaviors. For the sex addict who is raised in a religion
that teaches that one can only have sex when married,
then marriage as soon as possible becomes the focus in
life.

The woman quoted here had such a religious upbring-
ing, and she admits that she got married for sex—not
love!

Getting married for sex will never bring happiness.
Happiness will come when sex and love are intertwined.

*I understand the spiritual connection
between sex and love.*

Denial

My friend brags about his sex addiction.
He thinks it's funny.

Humor is often an ingredient of denial. I remember reading two quotes attributed, allegedly, to Winston Churchill concerning his drinking:

> Winston Churchill was having dinner with Lady Astor, when she suddenly exclaimed to him, "If I was your wife I'd poison your coffee!"
> Churchill replied, "If I was your husband, I'd drink it."

> Bessie Braddock from Liverpool once said to Churchill, "Winston, you're drunk!"
> Churchill replied, "Bessie, you're ugly, but in the morning I shall be sober."

Funny? Maybe. But Churchill's responses also convey an aspect of denial.

Addicts are known for making jokes about their behavior, which mostly serves only to hide the pain.

Today I have decided not to minimize
serious issues by using humor.

Reality

My therapist says that sex is beautiful. If she only knew!

When the therapist says that sex is beautiful, she is not referring to sex addiction or the numerous thoughts and actions that permeate sexual compulsivity. I suppose anything in life can be abused, damaged, or made ugly:

- Discourse is an aspect of freedom that enables creativity in all aspects of life. However, it can be twisted to create argument, hate, and prejudice.
- Food is a satisfying gift from God, but for the compulsive eater, bulimic, or anorexic, it becomes a vehicle for sickness and death.
- Alcohol is a refreshing and social gift to many people, but it can destroy the alcoholic and his or her loved ones.

Hopefully, one day the sex addict will also experience that sex is a precious gift from God. Sex truly is beautiful.

Today I'm able to discover God's love in my sexual expression toward others.

Acceptance

I've been in treatment for alcoholism six times. I've acknowledged my eating disorder, but I find it too shaming to discuss my sex addiction.

Here we see the fear that surrounds sex addiction. People who have been able to own and acknowledge other addictions reach a stone wall when it comes to their sex addiction. It seems almost impossible to get to the point of acceptance and recovery. Yet many people are doing just that. I often catch myself saying, "I can't do that," only to find later that I am doing exactly what I said I couldn't do. Time is a great healer.

An argument for placing alcoholics and people with eating disorders among sex addicts is that in the group sessions people listen to the stories of others, *and they can identify with them.*

Even the shame of sex addiction is overcome by an atmosphere of love, tolerance, and acceptance.

*I share my pain in my
spiritual program.*

Fantasy

I'm a mother who loves her teenage son. But I fantasize about having sex with him.

All professionals in the field of addiction suggest that being honest is a prerequisite for healing and recovery. I want to honor the mother quoted here for talking about something that is incredibly dark to talk about, let alone admit.

However, being honest about a fantasy is no substitute for receiving help and healing. We all have a dark side. Sexual fantasies, like all things sexual, are difficult to talk about, and incestuous thinking is among the most difficult to own. Yet the spiritual solution for all secrets and covert behavior is the same: *Begin the conversation.* Find a therapist with whom you are able to share your thoughts and fears, allowing yourself to be guided toward forgiveness and personal healing.

This topic is not easy to discuss, but failure to get help could be devastating for all concerned.

God, today I am willing to face and discuss my darkest secrets.

September

Anger

I'm HIV-positive. I'm also a sex addict.
I know the two are connected, and I'm so
angry at myself.

We know that sex addiction creates havoc in personal lives and relationships. It also can be the source of HIV and AIDS. I wonder how many sex addicts have lamented, "I'm so angry at myself."

The feeling of anger must be felt. It is okay to feel shame or guilt about a certain behavior or conversation, but it is never healthy to stay stuck in these feelings. Regardless of the behavior, a time comes when we must move on.

Spirituality always brings the possibility of change, and within this philosophy lies hope. People are living with HIV and AIDS. People are recovering from sex addiction and sexual compulsivity. Yes, many were angry, some full of rage at themselves. They worked through it. They got beyond it.

Today I can feel my anger, but
I know I am not my anger.

Spirituality

I see my work, my labor at the law office, as spiritual. My work in therapy for my sexual compulsivity is also spiritual.

I often say in my lectures that my work is how I play in life and my play usually involves work. I'm most fortunate in the work I do: I help alcoholics, addicts, and sex addicts get recovery and keep it. Occasionally it is depressing work, but most times it is uplifting, and it's always satisfying.

The work ethic in my family of origin was very healthy. I don't remember anybody being slothful. Perhaps that is why I'm able to find spirituality in almost everything I do. Labor Day is a spiritual celebration for me.

Yes, therapy, treatment, and recovery are work, but they are productive work, work that benefits me and all the people I love.

*Thank you, God, for
the gift of work.*

Violence

*I use sex to control my girlfriend. Sometimes
I punish her with brutal sex; other times I refuse
to touch her.*

When we study the pathology of sex addiction and sexual compulsivity, we often see how insecurity and control appear to be tragic symptoms, keeping the person trapped in sick relationships.

Before I entered recovery for my alcoholism, I was acutely aware of my self-loathing because of the behavior resulting from bouts of drunkenness. However, I invariably projected this self-hatred onto others. In my suffering, I made others suffer!

We know that the person quoted here is not happy about his behavior. What should he do? Get help. Sex addiction and sexual compulsivity are treatable, and support programs can be found in every major city. Unless an intervention takes place to enable a change in behavior, the abusiveness will continue.

*Today I do not make excuses for
my abusive behavior.*

Information

I've heard that sex addiction happens to people who, when they were children, didn't have sex education. They discovered sex on the streets.

It is certainly *not* true that *all* sex addicts didn't receive sex education when they were growing up. And many people who are *not* sex addicts didn't receive formal sex education from parents or school either and learned about sex on the streets. The truth is that many paths lead to sex addiction.

We are still learning some of the aspects of sex addiction. Some sex addicts, although their lives are unmanageable, are able to sustain intimate relationships, while others are loners and live isolated lives.

The foundation for treatment must always involve a spiritual message that affirms the dignity of sexuality. This will translate into respect for other people and self. It would be an important goal to have all children raised with this spiritual information.

*God, I know that spirituality
must involve respect.*

Rape

I definitely need help for my sex addiction.
I've had thoughts about raping a stranger—
and they're real thoughts!

I remember counseling a sex addict and hearing him reply that he would not share some of his thoughts with anyone. Some images were so horrid that he would not want to speak them aloud. The preceding quotation made me think about this person.

Thankfully, the person quoted here is asking for help. Recovery can begin only when he is willing to ask for help. I admire this person for being willing to be rigorously honest: "I've had thoughts about raping a stranger."

Spiritual surrender involves being honest—being willing not only to talk about the covert behavior but also to share the "secret thoughts."

God, I'm not proud of some of
my thoughts, but I'm willing to share
them to receive healing.

Sexual Manipulation

I force my wife to have sex, but she never seems to complain. Is it a game? I'm beginning to think it's rape.

A friend of mine, who is not in recovery, once commented that sex addicts were sick. He seemed disgusted when I shared the preceding quotation. Perhaps so few people receive treatment for sex addiction because they feel disgusted. Even sex addicts are disgusted with themselves. Religious judgmentalism has kept treatment and recovery in the shadows.

Yes, sex addicts are sick, unhealthy, and abusive to themselves and those they love—but so are all addicts. My alcoholism was certainly sick, and everyone, including myself, was disgusted at my behavior.

Addicts play games, as do loved ones, to maintain the denial. Fear, low self-esteem, rape, and sick behavior ensue.

Yet sex addiction is treatable. Recovery happens when the sex addict is able to overcome the disgusted feelings and embrace healing.

Spiritually, I was loved by others until I was able to love myself.

Predators

I watched a TV show about sexual predators.
I did the same things, only I didn't get caught.

I was made to realize the power of addiction, the absolute loss of control, when I watched a predator on a cable TV show. He had watched previous shows, and he was saying that he thought he might be being set up—and possibly arrested. He still went to see the young girl—and he *was* arrested.

The destructive power of sex addiction consumes a person's thinking, and the sex addict often takes insane risks. It is a sickness that disregards common sense, manipulates others, and occasionally breaks the law.

Still, there is spiritual healing, and hope and recovery are available. However, the sex addict must be willing to ask for help, attend Sex Addicts Anonymous (SAA) support groups, and possibly enter treatment.

Preventive healing is the antidote to tragedy.

Thank you for those occasional moments
of sanity, when I reached out for help.

Therapy

*My wife says I'm a sex addict. I think I'm
suffering from love addiction, and I have been
unfaithful numerous times.*

Many sex addicts would prefer to describe themselves as love addicts. It's less offensive, less sordid, and easier to discuss in polite company!

Can you be both? Yes. However *sex addiction* is not the same as *love addiction*.

Love addiction is more about being needy and only feeling happy when in a relationship. It's a romantic version of codependency.

Sex addiction is an obsession concerning sex. Even if you are not doing it, you are thinking about it or having fantasies about it. When the sex addict is active in the addiction, the sex is more important than the love.

In the preceding quotation we read, "I have been unfaithful numerous times." This indicates a sex addiction. When it is accepted for what it is, then healing and recovery can begin.

*Acceptance is an important ingredient
in my spiritual program.*

Atheism

I'm a sex addict in recovery. I'm also an atheist.
My 12 Step support groups welcome me.

The 12 Step program is spiritual, not religious. While it is certainly true that most people who attend meetings believe in God or a Higher Power, more than a few agnostics and atheists also attend meetings.

I've always suggested that everything in the 12 Step program must be interpreted and applied creatively to each person's situation.

This applies particularly to Step Three: Made a decision to turn our will and our lives over to the care of God *as we understood him.* We may prefer the care of a "Higher Power" or a "Divine Energy."

I know that the 12 Step program is for everyone because I've met almost every type of person in meetings over the years. However, it is often necessary to work with the language to feel comfortable.

An atheist often finds a spiritual power in the group, and that's okay.

My spiritual program is based
upon respect, never dogma.

Relapse

I've been in treatment for my alcoholism six times. Each time I've been sexually inappropriate with other patients. Could I be a sex addict?

When you say that you have been "sexually inappropriate" where you have had treatment for alcoholism, you are opening the door to the possibility that you are a sexual compulsive.

The alcoholic or drug addict often exhibits obsessive-compulsive behavior concerning sex. Years ago, sex addiction was not discussed. In recent years, therapists have been suggesting that an untreated sex addiction could easily be the "gateway behavior" to relapse.

When we refuse to confront a behavior that we know to be real, it is called "denial." Because of religious morals, severe judgmentalism concerning sexual behavior, or an emphasis on sinfulness, sex addiction is one of the last addictions to creep out of the closet. But it is real. And it is treatable. Thousands of sex addicts are enjoying recovery. The first step to healing is a willingness to ask for help.

Today I surrender to the fact that I've been sexually inappropriate because I'm a sex addict.

Shame

I feel sorry for sex addicts because they can't help it. They're just like alcoholics without the sympathy.

F̲ew people have the empathy expressed in the preceding quotation. Most people view the sex addict as a criminal who should be locked away.

Spiritually, however, it is important not to be locked into the idea that they can't help it; rather, the healing emphasis should be placed on what sex addicts can do about their behavior. It is not enough for the sex addict to live off the sympathy of others.

Writing as a recovering alcoholic, I know that it is possible to break away from negative thinking and destructive behavior and embrace treatment and recovery. We certainly *can* help the way we choose to live with an addiction.

When I accept that I am a sex addict,
I also embrace responsibility.

Abuse

I masturbated in front of a teenage boy on a train. He seemed to enjoy watching me. But I'm so ashamed.

Sex addiction—that uncontrollable compulsivity concerning sexual behavior—takes an individual into abusive and dangerous activities. Here we read about a sex addict masturbating in front of a teenage stranger in a public place. We see the reality of what the 12 Step program states in Step One: *We admitted we were powerless over addictive sexual behavior—that our lives had become unmanageable.*

A redeeming feature in this incident is that the person feels "so ashamed." Yet feeling shame is no substitute for getting help, entering therapy, and beginning a recovery program for serious sex addiction.

Pain is a common ingredient of most interventions. This shaming pain can lead to doing a personal intervention *on ourselves.*

*God, I thank you for my
feelings of shame.*

Ignorance

What is wrong with being a sex addict?
It's better than being impotent.

There is nothing wrong with being a sex addict, and there is nothing wrong with being impotent.

Spiritually, we grow when we can get away from thinking in terms of "right" or "wrong" and more toward what is healthy or unhealthy. We only add to our personal shame when we continue to see ourselves as "being wrong." We all have to face challenges throughout our lives, and being a sex addict is more a mental health issue than a moral one.

However, sex for many people is an embarrassing topic to discuss, whether it is impotence or sex addiction. Both can be excessively shaming.

Spiritually, we heal when we are able to face what is actually going on in our lives and accept it: not good or bad, not right or wrong. Comparisons of better or best, when it comes to health issues, are not helpful.

Today I understand that sexual challenges
are often mental health issues.
Moral judgments about them are not helpful.

Information

Does sexual abuse create sex addiction? My friend says it does—and I was sexually abused.

Some people who were sexually abused grow up to be sex addicts, but the emphasis must be placed on *some*. Not all those who were sexually abused grow up to be sex addicts. In fact, many sex addicts were never sexually abused.

It is good to listen to friends, but friends do not necessarily have a license to practice therapy. Sex addicts and their significant others are getting help in therapy and treatment, and nothing substitutes for seeing a professional.

When it comes to sex addiction, much misinformation and ignorance serve only to confuse people, often creating fear and feelings of hopelessness. Spiritual healing and ongoing support are available for the sex addict, as they are for other addictions, and these affirm hope and recovery.

Today I seek the truth and avoid hearsay and gossip.

Surrender

The horrors of my living as a sex addict were healed, relatively easily, once I made the decision to get help.

I often hear people say that it is difficult to get well, it is challenging to find recovery, it is not easy to heal from sex addiction.

Spiritually, I've come to believe that we often create what we say in our lives. If we keep saying that something is "hard" or "difficult," then that is exactly what it will be!

My recovery from alcoholism was easier than living as a drunk. Once I embraced the acceptance, the subsequent recovery was relatively easy. So it is for the person quoted here.

It is easier to get well than it is to stay sick. Yes, challenges must be faced, but the rewards are substantial: Existence is exchanged for real life.

*In recovery I'm responsible in the pleasure,
gentle in the enthusiasm, and
respectful in the desire.*

Sin

*I go to Sex Addicts Anonymous meetings.
I have four years of recovery—but I still cannot
forgive myself. I think I'm sinful.*

Religious morality has severely condemned many aspects of sexuality, driving the activity into secrecy and covert behavior. A person is made to feel so sinful that he or she could not possibly admit having a problem and feels too ashamed to ever talk about having a sex addiction.

This aspect of religious abuse colludes with the sickness, often keeping the sex addict in denial. I'm pleased to read in the preceding quotation that the person is going to SAA meetings; however, he or she is still unable to practice self-forgiveness. When we immerse ourselves in a spiritual program, breaking away from religious moral judgments, we are better able to accept our imperfections. Time is a great healer, and seeing a therapist might also prove to be a healing experience.

*Today I know that I make mistakes,
but I am not a mistake.*

Intervention

The hardest call I made was arranging an intervention for my son's sex addiction, but it went well, and he's now six years in recovery.

Intervention is a spiritual experience. An organized honesty is created within a group of people in order to confront the denial that often accompanies addiction.

It is not easy to intervene in the life of a person whom we love. We often fear how our loved one will respond. We imagine violent arguments and upsets, perhaps anticipating that the person will storm out of the room.

This does happen, but most interventions are successful because they confront not only the denial but the pain that exists in the addict's life. Yes, the addict is in pain and hates the feelings of powerlessness and unmanageability. The addict lives with fear daily.

A spiritual intervention offers freedom. Recovery from sex addiction allows for the possibility of loving relationships.

Hearing the truth from loved ones was my wake-up call.

Obsession

When I'm away from home I always track down a gentleman's club in the area. I'm addicted to these clubs.

I t is something of a cliché to say that addiction substitutes a life of mere existence for the living of a vibrant life. What a tragedy to imagine this man driving around for hours while searching out a gentleman's club to feed his addiction.

As a recovering alcoholic, I often reflect upon the amount of time I wasted in my addiction—the lost days and evenings, the fear and anxiety of knowing that I was out of control—and sex addiction is no different.

The solution is recovery. The solution is therapeutic healing. Easier said than done, you might say. Maybe. But it is the emotional pain of being out of control that usually leads an addict to seek help. Recovery is available.

Today I choose to live my life
rather than to merely exist.

Manipulation

Sex is a gift from God. How can it be addictive?

Almost anything in this life can be abused. We can abuse power, money, food, alcohol, people, relationships, work—and sex.

I think most of us know this to be true, but that does not take us away from the point made in the preceding quotation: *Sex is a gift from God.*

Sex, like the many ingredients that make up life, is a most precious gift from God, or Higher Power, that enables the expression of deep love. It also excites and feeds certain relationships. Because of the natural "euphoria" it creates, it can become addictive.

It is affirmed that sex addiction can be healed, that treatment and recovery are available for that purpose.

Thank you, Great Spirit, for the gift of a healthy sexuality.

Irresponsibility

*I'm an irresponsible, single parent. I've let my
teenage children have sex in the house. Sometimes
I even encourage it.*

One has to admire a person who is willing to pull his
or her own cover and state unequivocally, "I'm an
irresponsible, single parent." Owning and acknowledging unhealthy behavior mark the beginning of change,
the beginning of pursuing the spiritual life.

The key to actually living the spiritual life is the willingness to change. In response to the preceding quotation, the focus must be on changing the irresponsible
behavior that involves sex.

Dysfunctional sexual attitudes and behaviors are very
complicated and often have their roots in childhood.
Creating a spiritual life often involves the parent, who
was once a child, being willing to seek help and begin
developing healthy boundaries. The family might also
benefit from meeting with a therapist to begin discussing
what a healthy home might look like.

*God, I truly understand that as a parent I am
responsible for the messages I give my children.*

The Chase

I am a sex addict who loves the chase.
I get "high" from selecting a stranger and
seeing if I can have sex with him.

Euphoria is often connected with sex addiction: it's the *high* that feeds the addiction and stimulates the chase. Naturally, this can often create tremendous risks, both personal and legal. It also reveals a complete lack of respect for the person who is pursued simply for sex and treated like an object or commodity.

When we seek to develop a spiritual life, a core ingredient is respect for self and others. We embrace a positive and creative life that celebrates love and a joy that is discovered in old and new relationships.

Sex addiction, because of its use of other people, destroys the possibility of healthy and respectful relationships. However, sex addicts can change their destructive behavior, get help, join a recovery program, and, if necessary, enter treatment. We must never lose sight of the hope for healing.

Today it is not acceptable
for me to use people.

Humility

Why can't I just admit I'm a sexual compulsive and go to my church? Why do I need therapy?

Some people experience recovery and healing by attending their church, especially if their church has recovery support groups. I certainly don't want to limit the power of God in a person's life or the healing power of prayer.

For many people, however, church is not enough. They must be able to talk specifically about their sex addiction and receive advice and support from fellow addicts or therapists.

I've often said that there are many paths to God, and there are many paths to healing and recovery. It is important, though, to have the humility to know when a certain way is not working out for you and to be willing to accept another path.

*God, I know there are many
paths to healing.*

Codependency

I've been married three times, each time to a sex addict. Am I codependent?

Just as it is presumptuous to say who is an alcoholic or sex addict—it's much better for addicts to look at the symptoms and diagnose themselves—it is not for me to determine if the person in the preceding quotation is a codependent.

However, when we read, "I've been married three times, each time to a sex addict," we know something is out of balance.

An addict usually exhibits certain behaviors that would make a healthy person suspicious, especially if you had experiences, through a previous marriage, that revealed unmanageability and powerlessness.

Codependents are often needy, believing even when confronted by unacceptable behavior that they can change or fix a person. The results are usually disastrous.

The spiritual healing for codependents includes developing a program of self-love and establishing healthy boundaries.

Today, I affirm healthy relationships.

Compulsive Sexual Behavior

I'm a compulsive masturbator. Also, I'm always looking at pornography. But does this make me a sex addict?

We know that addiction is defined as a lack of balance. Compulsive eaters are always obsessing about food, drug addicts are constantly seeking drugs, and the sex addict is consumed with things sexual.

We read here about an addict who is a compulsive masturbator and is *always* looking at pornography. Those behaviors indicate a clear lack of balance.

I suggest that this person consult a therapist or attend a Sex Addicts Anonymous (SAA) meeting. Spiritually, it is never a good idea to tell a person he or she is a sex addict. It's better for the addict to confront his or her denial, which, hopefully, will eventually lead to full acceptance of Step One: *We admitted we were powerless over addictive sexual behavior—that our lives had become unmanageable.*

*I am spiritually free when
I know who I am.*

Sexual Objectifying

When I'm talking to attractive women, I'm thinking about sex. Sometimes I forget what we're talking about.

It is not unusual, when we are in conversation with attractive, beautiful people, to lose our concentration. The fact that we forget momentarily what we are talking about is not a sign of addiction. However, the red flag in the preceding quotation is the statement, "When I'm talking to attractive women, I'm thinking about sex."

Thinking about sex does not necessarily indicate a sex addiction, but constantly thinking about sex, or sexualizing many of the people we meet in a day, could be a sign that we have crossed into sex addiction. Eventually, the addiction would affect our work and personal relationships.

Attending a few Sex Addicts Anonymous (SAA) groups might be helpful, exposing us to the experience of acknowledged sex addicts, the nature of the program, and the diversity of people involved.

Because of my belief in the impeccability of the word, I seek to be present in my conversations.

Denial

*I would never admit to being a sex addict—
even if I knew I was!*

What a sad statement to read. I've known many alcoholics who died from their alcoholism rather than admit they had a problem. Their shame, guilt, and fear blocked their recovery. Others were simply unwilling to change their behavior, even though that behavior was creating chaos in their lives.

Sex is a powerful force in our society. It has become, particularly pornography, a billion-dollar business. And some people love this addiction—to death!

Some people change when the pain created by the sex addiction becomes too great. Family members get involved, legal issues develop, and the unmanageability can no longer be tolerated.

Many sex addicts and their loved ones are healing. Hope is affirmed. It all begins when we admit we have a problem.

*God, I can no longer live
with my denial.*

Generalizations

*Since attending SA and SLAA meetings, I think
everyone is a sex addict. I see them everywhere!*

It is certainly true that many sex addicts live in the
world. However, *not everyone* is a sex addict!

Recovery from alcoholism is an essential part of my
life. Most of my friends are in recovery. And, yes, it often
feels like everyone is a recovering alcoholic, but they are
not. Our lives do become compartmentalized, but not
everyone lives in the same compartment. In truth, many
people enjoy a drink of wine and have no problems.

Diversity and variety are important components of
spirituality. We all have different gifts, different ideas
about God and the meaning of life. It all adds to the
richness of living. We are not the same.

*Today I embrace the
variety of life.*

Flirting

I love having sex. If I like a man I flirt.
Sometimes I stare at his crotch. However,
I couldn't go on with this behavior. That's why
I got help.

I remember talking with the woman quoted here, and I was touched by the shame and anxiety she exhibited. She seemed to know that had she not gotten help—she was involved in a treatment center for sex addiction and alcoholism—things would only get worse.

But she was receiving help. She was *doing something* about her unmanageable behavior.

Spirituality has never been about being perfect. We are not God, but spirituality does involve a willingness to cooperate with the Divine Spirit to bring about healing in our lives. People *are* healing and recovering. Sex Addicts Anonymous (SAA) groups exist around the world, and people are reclaiming their lives one day at a time.

I surrender when I ask for help.

Gratitude

My treatment for sex addiction has changed my life. I'm a new woman. And I'm so grateful.

Treatment works. I know this to be true in my personal recovery from alcoholism, and I see it happening in the lives of many sex addicts.

Treatment often involves the willingness to sit with a professional or another recovering addict to get honest—*rigorously honest*.

Spiritually, I've come to understand that many people lie by omission, by what they don't say, rather than by what they do say. It is the lie of silence.

Only when we are honest about what is happening can we change. Then a spiritual awakening occurs, a new life is realized, and gratitude becomes a daily response.

I am grateful for being given the ability to see what must change and then to do it.

Therapy

I know I'm a love addict, but I really don't want to think that I'm a sex addict. Tell me they are not interchangeable—please.

Love addiction and sex addiction are definitely not interchangeable. Many people are love addicts, with a consuming neediness to be in a relationship. Others are definitely sex addicts, compulsive and obsessive about sex, not love. And because people are very complex, some people are both love addicts and sex addicts.

The interesting part of the preceding quotation is "but I really don't want to think that I'm a sex addict." Because of the tremendous shame associated with all things sexual, the thought of being a sex addict is almost too much for some people to face. Denial is rampant with most addicts, especially sex addicts; hence, few are getting help.

Spirituality often involves facing the reality of our lives, seeing who we are and not who we want to be. It takes courage to admit to being a sex addict; it also takes courage to admit to being a love addict.

*An aspect of spirituality
is facing reality.*

Information

My son plays with himself. He's ten years old.
His father, who I divorced, is a sex addict.
Does sex addiction run in families, like
alcoholism does?

I'm not aware of any psychiatrist who would suggest that sex addiction is genetic, that such a gene can be passed down from one family member to another. However, children are influenced by the behavior of their parents, and it is possible that the son cited here is imitating what he saw his father doing. Also, if the son watches certain singers, he might observe them grabbing their crotch. Human beings, including children, are influenced by what they see other people doing.

However, it is not unusual for young children to "play with themselves," and it would be unwise to suggest that a ten-year-old boy is a sex addict. Healthy sex information and teaching about social boundaries would be helpful for the future.

Spiritually, I believe it is important to teach my children healthy and respectful social interaction.

Sexual Anorexia

My therapist says I'm a sexual anorexic. In treatment I called myself a sex addict. Can you be both?

The profile of the sexual anorexic varies, but they tend to be loners, people who find it difficult to open up with another human being, and they constantly experience challenges and intimacy issues.

A key ingredient of treatment requires the spiritual component, which I define as being a positive and creative human being. This requires the willingness to share covert behavior and secrets that have never been told to anyone. Healing begins with confronting guilt and shame and progresses gently into self-forgiveness.

Support groups, such as Sex Addicts Anonymous (SAA), are extremely helpful in getting the sexual anorexic to experience recovery by listening to others share their feelings of loneliness: what happened, what they felt, what they feel now. Thousands of people are recovering due to their willingness to open up.

I know my healing involves confronting my loneliness and feelings of isolation.

Support

My family had an open attitude about sex issues.
This helped me confront my sex addiction and
seek help. I'm not ashamed for having a sickness.

Few families are able to talk together easily, and so the family described in the preceding quotation is to be commended. Shame is the enemy of help and treatment for the sex addict. This shame leads to covert behavior.

As with all addictions, the more sex addiction is talked about and explained in mental health terms, rather than condemned with moral dictates, the more the sex addict and his or her significant other will get the help they need.

Spiritual healing comes with honesty. It is important, therefore, for those of us who are professionals in the addiction field to create a nonjudgmental atmosphere in which sex addicts can discuss their behavior and *not* feel ashamed for having a sickness.

Today I celebrate
my recovery from shame.

Information

Is sex addiction another way of talking about oversexed people?

When we begin to discuss sex addiction and sexual compulsivity, we realize that it is "cunning, baffling, and powerful," and that because it is relatively new to the general public it can easily be caricatured.

What does *oversexed* mean? Is it having a strong sexual drive, or does it describe a person who is consumed, obsessed with sex? Having a strong sex drive is healthy and an important aspect of establishing healthy intimate relationships. Being consumed by sexual thoughts or behaviors, however, is probably related to addiction, and it would benefit us to admit that we have become powerless (dysfunctional) because of sex and that our lives have become unmanageable.

A healthy spirituality always includes sexuality that emphasizes a balanced and respectful sexual expression.

Great Spirit, I celebrate my balanced sexuality.

Spirituality

I'm a sex addict. How do I become spiritual?

Part of living the spiritual life involves knowing who we are and what constitutes our personality. Knowing you are a sex addict is a step in the right direction.

Denial has often been seen as the enemy of living the spiritual life. Denial is not the same as ignorance: *ignorance* is when we don't know something; *denial* is when we know but refuse to accept.

Some people feel that to be spiritual we must live a perfect life. I do not believe this. However, it is important to be honest about what is happening in our lives as we seek to heal our woundedness. Knowing you are a sex addict is the beginning of enlightenment; doing something about it is wisdom.

Today I accept my sex addiction,
but I also pursue healing
and recovery.

Sex Addiction

*I think about sex all the time. I sexualize
everyone. I even do it at church.*

As we have seen in recent years concerning "clergy
abuse," you cannot keep sex addiction out of any
aspect of life—and this includes the church.

A symptom of sex addiction is when we move beyond
finding a person beautiful or attractive and sexualize
them. We picture them naked, doing something with
others or ourselves, and we become consumed by their
anatomy. Spiritually, we do not see the full perspective of
who the person is because we have focused on their
sexual parts.

The beauty of human beings lies in their complexity:
the many aspects of being human that make up the personality. This is lost on the sex addict, who not only is a
prisoner of his or her thoughts but also must confine and
restrain others, thereby losing track of others' spiritual
essence. The miracle of being human is then down-
graded to sex!

*Today I celebrate the spiritual complexity
that makes us human.*

Confusion

I think my openness about sex has led to me being a sexual compulsive.

I don't think that being open about sex leads to becoming a sex addict or sexual compulsive. Openness is an aspect of spirituality; it speaks of a willingness to see all aspects of an issue and a willingness to accept that sexual expression often differs from one person to the next.

The seeds of sex addiction often are guilt and shame. Fearing sex or being told that sexuality, outside of marriage, is inherently sinful often leads to covert behavior and secrets: *the exact opposite of openness.*

It is not enough to know that you behave compulsively concerning sex, but you must be willing to seek help and possible treatment.

Today I connect being responsible with a healthy sexuality.

Dishonesty

I was divorced because my wife found out
I used prostitutes. Now I'm dating—and I'm
still using prostitutes. Should I get help?

A person usually seeks help when he or she accepts having a problem. It is a personal decision that often revolves around personal happiness. I'm assuming from the preceding quotation that the woman does not know that he is using prostitutes. If she knew, then presumably the behavior that had created the earlier divorce would probably lead to a breakup.

Sex addiction is enmeshed in a life of lies, deceit, and covert behavior. It is never the spiritual life because it is dishonest. Most people see that sex addiction is a behavior that leads to a tragic life lived on the edge.

Only the individual who is suffering sexual compulsivity can make the decision to seek help. Spiritually, it is important to know that help is available.

My spiritual program does not allow
for lies or deceitful behavior.

Abusive Masturbation

*I masturbate so much that sometimes my
penis is blistered.*

We know that sex addiction creates mental anxiety
and emotional despair, but it also can have physical consequences. We can do serious damage to our
bodies.

Compulsive masturbation is a symptom of sex addiction. Constantly acting out creates its own drama and
often leads to isolation. Because sexual behavior, especially masturbation, can be embarrassing to talk about
for many people, the shame created by *compulsive* masturbation feeds the need for isolation.

I think the preceding quotation is a scream for help,
and help is most certainly available. Hope and recovery
are available for the sex addict. The first step is to begin
the conversation with a therapist who can assist. Often,
in this area of addiction, we discover that in order to live
the spiritual life, therapy will be involved.

*Great Spirit, I'm discovering the power
of spiritual healing in therapy.*

Inappropriate Behavior

*Occasionally I play with myself when I'm in
meetings. I've been confronted at work about
my behavior, but I do it all the time.*

The 12 Step program, which is the basis for ongoing
support and recovery for sex addiction, clearly states
that we have a problem when we are experiencing powerlessness and unmanageability. To occasionally "play
with yourself" is healthy and not a problem; however,
to continue to "play with yourself" after being confronted at work about your behavior is surely an indica-
tor of *powerlessness* and *unmanageability*.

Usually a person does not change behavior until there
are consequences. Maybe termination or legal proceed-
ings are necessary to get the attention of the person
quoted here.

It is also spiritually disrespectful to sexually invade the
space of another person. A key ingredient of the spiritual
life is establishing healthy boundaries.

*God, I understand the selfishness involved
in not respecting healthy boundaries.*

Unmanageable

*I'm a married man. Recently my sex addiction
led to my having sex with my best friend's wife.
Now I'm flirting with my sister-in-law. Occasionally I go to SAA meetings, but I still act out.*

I remember hearing a therapist say that staying in a
treatment center is not treatment, that treatment
happens when we are willing to confront the shadows in
our lives, discuss the possible sources of our guilt and
shame, and begin the process of incremental change—
one day at a time.

Attending a Sex Addicts Anonymous (SAA) meeting is not recovery. It is only when we seek to implement
the 12 Step program, activate the steps in our life, and
surrender to the concept of healing—one day at a time—
that recovery begins to take place.

The preceding quotation reveals a person who is disregarding the recommendations that are the core ele-
ments of the 12 Step program. Change is required if
disaster is to be avoided.

*My Higher Power is teaching me that
action must follow intention.*

Slippery Slope

I rubbed against a young woman on the subway.
She moved away. Nothing happened.
Now I want to do it again.

Unless consequences develop from our unhealthy and abusive behavior, the dysfunction will continue. If an addict gets away with what he or she has done, the addictive behavior will probably continue.

Sex addiction is not simply an abuse of self. It often involves an active abuse and manipulation of others, a covert behavior embarked upon for selfish gratification. This behavior will continue until an intervention stops the behavior and affirms treatment, healing, and recovery.

The spiritual program affirms personal healing, and it involves establishing respectful boundaries, along with a respect for self. It also establishes a process that enables a change in destructive and abusive behavior.

My program of change involves
a spiritual foundation.

Shame

I've never told anybody that I'm a sex addict.
I'm thinking about sex all the time, but I'm so
ashamed.

I've often felt that it is almost impossible to treat sex addiction without looking at the systematic aspects of religious abuse that create the guilt, shame, and fear. Until we can move a client away from feeling bad or sinful, it is almost impossible to develop the rigorous honesty that will lead to treatment and healing. I know, from talking with hundreds of sex addicts who were also alcoholic, that it was harder for them to open up about their sex addiction than their alcoholism. Toxic messages were often experienced in childhood and resulted in it being impossible to have a sensible conversation concerning sexuality; humor and jokes became the substitute.

The shame is being forced out of the shadows, and many sex addicts are receiving treatment and attending 12 Step Sex Addicts Anonymous (SAA) support groups.

Today I know that God does not consider me
disgusting. I am a precious child of God.

Education

I didn't know sex addiction covered so many things, until I went to SAA meetings. The stories are so comprehensive.

Isn't that the truth! Sex Addicts Anonymous (SAA) meetings are home for people who are *real* sex addicts, as well as romance and love addicts, sexual anorexics (who are often able to have sex but without any intimacy), and those who don't have sex but are still obsessive about it. I'm sure there are countless others.

Sex is complicated. The more we talk about it, the more we see how sweeping people's needs and desires tend to be.

For more than a few people, the spiritual dimension does not stop them from being sexually dysfunctional and abusive. Yet it is the spiritual component that brings healing and recovery: becoming that positive and creative human being who will facilitate the treatment that leads to change.

Today my spiritual program embraces diversity and simplicity.

Support Groups

*I'm married to a sex addict. She has no
intention of getting help. Are there support
groups for spouses?*

Many spouses and friends of sex addicts are being
helped in spiritual support groups connected with
12 Step programs. COSA is the Al-Anon of Sex
Addicts Anonymous (SAA); S-Anon is for family and
friends of Sexaholics Anonymous (SA); CoSLA is for
friends and family of Sex and Love Addicts Anonymous
(SLAA); and CoSC is for family and friends of Sexual
Compulsives Anonymous (SCA).

Addiction is a family disease. Like alcoholism, it
affects those who love the addict.

It is difficult to maintain a spiritual foundation for any
relationship with an addict if the addict refuses to get help,
refuses to change.

Recovery for the spouse is a process that inevitably
leads to a change in thinking and behaving.

*God, I understand that sometimes love is
not enough to maintain a marriage.*

Sexual Anorexia

I have a girlfriend, but we are hardly intimate.
I fear showing feelings. I think it might be
connected with my childhood: I was a loner.

It is probably impossible to have a healthy relationship
without the sacred ingredient of intimacy: the willingness to drop the guard and *be known*. Dr. Patrick
Carnes and other professionals who treat sex addictions
call this behavior *sexual anorexia*—a person who is able
to have sex while controlling their emotional vulnerability. It is usually expressed in a take-charge sexual behavior: *doing things rather than being present.*

Rigid religious teachings that taught that sex was
dirty or sinful, parents who rarely expressed feelings, a
society that seems to celebrate sexual conquests—all can
play a role in creating the sex addict and sexual anorexic.

The spiritual program of healing will involve a gentle
exploration of these dysfunctional messages, replacing
them with positive attitudes about sex and what makes
a healthy relationship.

My spiritual healing will involve
revisiting and healing my inner child.

Honesty

I cannot do the amends in the 12 Step program. They would send me to prison.

It is important to remember that the 12 Step program only *suggests*. It is made clear in Step Nine that some amends might not be helpful.

Step Nine: *"Made direct amends to such people wherever possible, except when to do so would injure them or others."*

Maybe it would be possible to make amends to a Higher Power through a sponsor, clergy, or a trusted friend. Some people, in recovery, have felt that in order to be rigorously honest they must "turn themselves in" to a police department; others take a different path.

I've often recommended that a person write down what he or she has said or done, pray and meditate over this written confession, alone or with friends, and then burn it.

Today I express my forgiveness in my forgiveness of others.

Common Sense

I like sex. That doesn't make me a sex addict.

A sex addict is not a person who likes sex. Indeed, I've met some sex addicts and compulsives who say they *don't* like sex. A healthy spirituality must incorporate our sexuality; it is a divine and essentially healthy energy given by God or Higher Power.

However, sex addiction is an abuse of this gift. It hurts the individual who has the addiction and wounds family and friends. It creates feelings of powerlessness and eventually results in unmanageable behavior. Sex addiction is unhealthy.

Shakespeare wrote, "Methinks he doth protest too much," and I sense this in the preceding quotation. One thing is certainly clear, and that is that sex addiction, alongside other addictions, is progressive—if it's addiction.

I celebrate sex, and I seek
to heal sex addiction.

Cynicism

I think treatment for sex addiction is another
way to make money. They should grow up
and take some responsibility for their lives—
or go to prison.

An alcoholic, who was in treatment for his alcoholism alongside some people who also suffered from sex addiction, shared this opinion with me. I pointed out that not too many years ago, the same opinion was being expressed by many people about those who suffered from alcoholism!

All sex addicts need help and support. Some are able to find what they need in Sex Addicts Anonymous (SAA) groups. Others definitely need treatment or therapy. Regardless, it is a sickness that is being healed, one day at a time.

Prison has never been the answer for addicts; in my opinion, it is a complete waste of time and money.

Today I accept that not everybody
accepts sex addiction as a sickness; spiritually,
I do not have to agree with everybody.

Acceptance

I was in a treatment center for addiction, and they had sex addicts and pedophiles in the group. I felt uncomfortable.

We already know that sex addiction invariably creates tremendous guilt and shame for those addicted; it also creates fear in society. Other addicts often are fearful or feel uncomfortable around sex addicts, *and they feel fear and contempt about pedophiles.*

It is okay to feel uncomfortable. It is also okay to express these feelings. However, all people should be treated by the professional with dignity and respect. Treatment centers and therapists exist to help and support "the wounded."

I have personally been helped by the honest sharing and stories of many sex addicts and pedophiles: It has been a spiritual experience.

I seek to love and respect all people, but I do not need to condone or agree with their behavior.

Gratitude

Is it strange to say that I'm seeing my AIDS as a gift from God? It has led to my living a spiritual life—in recovery.

I cannot tell you how many times in recovery meetings I've heard, "I'm glad I'm an alcoholic." Some continue to qualify this statement by saying that they may not be happy that they have the disease of alcoholism but are genuinely glad that they *know* they have it!

Not everyone would be able to consider their having AIDS as a gift from God, but the result of accepting their disease has led many people to incredible life changes. I've heard many share that only when they were able to face and embrace AIDS were they able to spiritually comprehend suffering and vulnerability. Some have shared their comfort ability with their own mortality; they accept death as an aspect of life and are not afraid.

Spiritual growth is often discovered in how we respond to a challenge in life.

In my recovery challenges,
I've discovered spiritual hope.

Therapy and Education

Can you be a love addict and a sex addict?
It's too confusing.

I've always found it helpful to say that sex can be an important part of love, and a loving relationship often involves sex—but sex is not love and love is not sex.

Some people *are* sex addicts and love addicts, but the two addictions are not the same.

Sex addiction is really about sex, not romance. The sickness revolves around the sexual performance or the obsessive thinking about or looking at sexual situations. Historically, it has been difficult to discuss because of the religious judgments that have kept sexual behavior covert and secretive.

The love addict often will exchange sex for the possibility of a romantic relationship. Fear of being alone propels the love addict into unhealthy encounters. The solution, for both addictions, is healthy boundaries and a personal respect of self that does not fear asking for help.

Spiritually, I understand that honesty
often clears my confusion.

God

*I didn't believe in God when I entered treatment
for my sex addiction. Now I believe in a
Higher Power.*

Treatment is about change. Therapy is about change.
And the change for an addict, including a sex addict,
will necessarily be considerable.

It is also undeniably true that the 12 Step program,
which has never promoted itself as treatment and is
essentially support, has nevertheless had a tremendous
influence upon what happens in the treatment process.

The emphasis is upon spirituality in the 12 Steps,
rather than on religion, and the term *Higher Power* is
used for those who have a "problem" with "God." Many
agnostics and atheists have become comfortable with
that term. Higher Power is often associated with the
spiritual experience discovered in group sharing.

Some people have progressed from being comfortable
with Higher Power to a belief in God, and some have
returned to their house of worship.

*I experience God or Higher Power in the honest
sharing discovered in my support group.*

Hope

Today I live with AIDS . I tell people at my SAA meeting that the disease is a consequence of my compulsive sexual behavior. I'm trying to help others, but maybe it's too late!

It's never too late. I often hear tremendous courage expressed by people who attend recovery meetings. They willingly share information that might help the listener.

Sharing, rather than preaching, is a spiritual principle in 12 Step programs. People embrace a rigorous honesty that clearly states what happened, what it was like, and what it is like now. What happened to me need not happen to you. My consequences need not be yours.

This is the foundation of self-help meetings. We are willing to share our experiences, and together we can all grow.

Honest sharing can never come too late!

When I offer help to others,
I'm invariably helping myself.

Reality

*The intervention for my husband's sex addiction
did not work. However, it worked for me. I now
attend SLAA meetings for my love addiction.
And yes, we're divorced.*

In the preceding quotation, we hear something that is
often neglected: Addiction affects the family.

The sex addict often rejects help or does not feel that
help is needed. However, one result of a spiritual intervention—during which the addict is confronted with the
truth—is that family members or friends realize that *they*
need help. They realize that living with a sex addict has
caused problems in their lives, and therefore they decide
to see a therapist or attend a support group *for themselves*.

It is not only the sex addict who must make some
decisions but also family members and friends.

*Intervention will always affect
and possibly change the
family dynamic.*

Help

*Can you do an intervention for sex addiction?
I've heard that intervention really works for
alcoholics.*

An intervention can certainly be done for sex
addiction.

It is helpful to ask "What is an intervention?" During
an intervention, an addict is confronted by the truth of
his or her sickness, at a time when it is undeniable that,
unless the addict changes and gets help, the situation will
get worse.

An intervention need not involve loved ones giving a
"tough love" message. It might occur due to an unplanned
event: for example, an arrest for sexual misconduct, con-
tracting a sexually transmitted disease, or the shameful
realization about the type of material being viewed compulsively on the Internet.

An intervention occurs when a person is confronted
by a spiritual reality, and this is necessary in healing sex
addiction.

*A friend honestly shared her feelings with me,
and I heard her concern. That's intervention.*

Courage

I'm a married man with an active sex addiction.
I tend to solicit prostitutes. And I'm afraid to get
an HIV test. Any advice?

I think most addicts, even those who have some years in recovery, have experienced fear when it comes to being tested for HIV. This is certainly true for those who are still engaging in risky and irresponsible sexual behavior.

Recovery from sex addiction requires an honest admission that a problem exists. The dishonesty of being married and soliciting prostitutes must be confronted. Taking responsibility for our unhealthy attitudes and behaviors is an essential step in living a spiritual program.

My advice would be to see a therapist skilled in treating sex addiction and begin attending Sex Addicts Anonymous (SAA) support meetings. Get an HIV test—immediately!

Spiritually, I understand that when I ask
for advice I'm really asking for help.

Sexual Anorexia

I have no desire for intimacy. I just enjoy sex.
Does this make me a sexual anorexic?

The answer to the preceding question is "probably." What is interesting, from a spiritual perspective, is why a person has no desire for intimacy.

As a recovering alcoholic, I have friends who attend support meetings and also have a problem with establishing intimacy, or they feel that they don't need it. During my work in treatment centers, I observed that often something had happened in the childhood of an addict to create a pattern of withdrawal, a breaking away of any spiritual connection with other people. The sexual anorexic often will say that he or she still enjoys sex but is unable to or wishes to avoid intimacy.

In recovery, we often find that people's attitudes toward relationships change. They realize that being known on a spiritual level is missing in their lives, and they work on allowing themselves to be open and vulnerable.

My recovery program allows for intimacy and
vulnerability in my relationships.

Control

I have a serious control issue when it comes to sex. I prefer to pay for it. I get off on people owing me.

I've always understood spirituality to involve a certain vulnerability: knowing that *we are not God* and allowing for the fact that we all make mistakes. However, *we are not a mistake!*

In any healthy relationship we must allow people, especially those with whom we are in a significant relationship, to have the freedom to develop their own personalities.

The preceding quotation comes from a person who needs to control other people—hence his preference for prostitutes. As he said, "I get off on people owing me."

Most therapists would say that healthy sexual relationships affirm a spontaneity based upon respect and freedom. Treatment for the sex addict always encourages letting go of control for ongoing recovery and healing.

> *Today I seek to confront and
> heal my control issues.*

Low Self-Esteem

I've not had sex with a "real" person for years.
I know why: a girl laughed at the size of my
penis. Today I use the Internet and magazines.

We rarely discuss the issues that surround addiction without discussing shame. Shame creates a feeling of separation, inferiority, being "less than."

Therapists who treat sex addiction often remark about feelings of insecurity that characterize their clients. Secrecy and covert behavior are the result.

Because of the shaming remark concerning the size of his penis, the man quoted here has separated himself from people, reducing his sexual stimulation to the Internet and magazines. How sad! How tragic!

Hopefully, should this person seek help in Sex Addicts Anonymous (SAA) or therapy, he will discover the spiritual healing that comes with self-acceptance, healing the shame, and beginning the journey into an empowering self-love.

Today I accept the beauty of who I am.

Ghosts

Halloween night! Ghosts! Demons! Scary times!
Tonight I will go to my sex addiction meeting,
and I'll hear stories that reveal the "sexual
ghosts" of yesterday. They were scary times.
Today I'm embracing recovery and healing.

I enjoy horror movies. I enjoy reading horror and murder mysteries. I enjoy, for a short period of time, the feelings of terror and fear.

But facing *real* horror is something different. When I confronted my alcoholism, I was really afraid: afraid for my future, what people might think of me, what might happen to me. Alcohol was my cancer.

This is also true for sex addiction. Indeed, I feel it is more scary, more fearful to face because of the toxic shame that surrounds sex.

Yet thousands of men and women face their demons on a daily basis. My hat is off to them.

I embrace the gift of courage in my
spiritual battle with addiction.

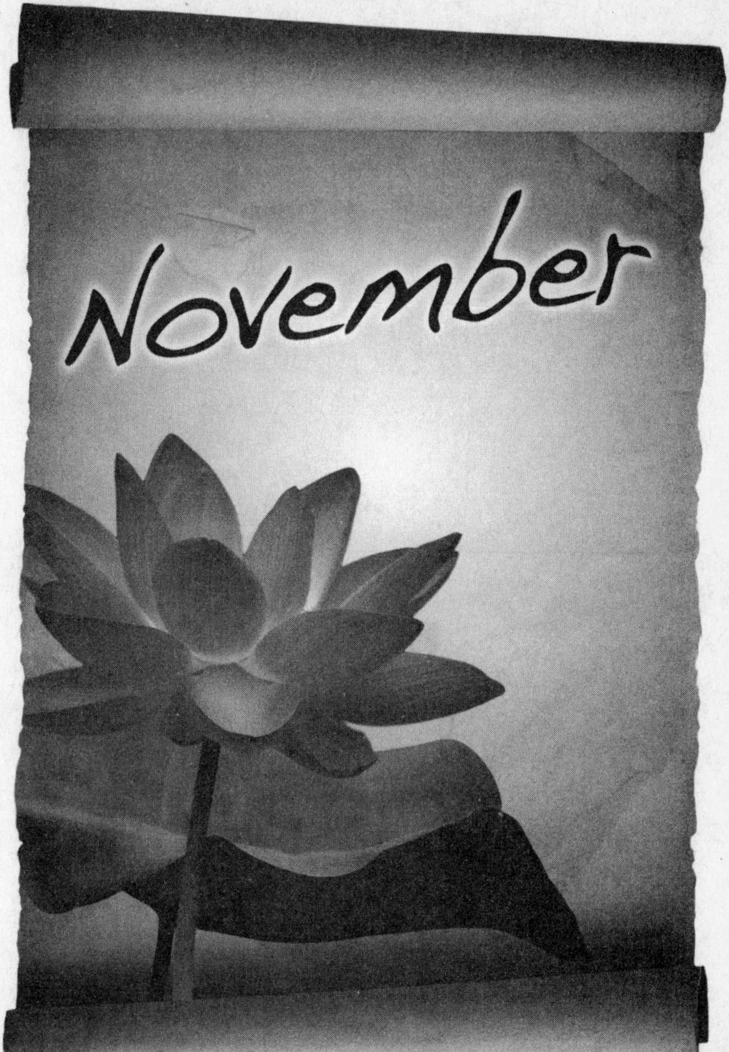
November

Education

A friend suggested I might be a sexual anorexic. What does this mean?

Sexual anorexia is a relatively new term that is being used to explain the behavior of those sexual compulsives who find it difficult to create intimacy in any of their relationships. Many sex addicts, although dysfunctional, are able to establish a level of intimacy with some people, but the sexual anorexic is isolated, a loner.

In his research, Dr. Patrick Carnes, an authority on sex addiction, has established that the *lost child syndrome* is often developed in childhood. At some point the sexual anorexic separates from people, and although able to perform sex, he or she is unable to be intimate.

However, healing and recovery are possible after intense therapy that revisits wounded childhood experiences. The treatment often focuses on an aspect of spirituality that seeks to develop connection and vulnerability. For the sexual anorexic, allowing other people into their lives is the key to a spiritual awakening.

My spiritual program encourages me to make a healthy connection with other people.

Shame

I masturbate, alone. I have a scar on my breast, and I feel ashamed. I feel ugly. I can't be intimate.

It is difficult to know, from the preceding quotation, if this is an issue of sex addiction or compulsion. However, it reveals a dysfunctional behavior that revolves around shame and the inability to be intimate.

Over time, I have defined for myself a definition of spirituality that is based upon being a *positive* and *creative* human being. When you feel ugly, it is difficult to be positive and creative.

This woman must address the isolation and insecurity resulting from the scar on her breast. I believe that spiritual healing will require therapy and possibly a nurturing support group.

Most of us experience some insecurity and personal challenges in our lives, but the *Say Yes to Your Sexual Healing* philosophy involves an awareness that spiritual healing exists within us and that occasionally we must seek beyond ourselves and ask for help.

I begin to heal my shame when
I seek the support of others.

Intimacy

My best sex is with prostitutes. Is something wrong with me?

Sex addiction is not about right or wrong. Sexual healing involves a willingness to confront unhealthy behaviors and create spiritual health and healing.

From my many consultations with sex addicts, I've learned that avoidance of intimacy is a common symptom. Controlling factors expressed in sexual behavior, particularly the use of prostitutes, with the other person becoming a *commodity* or *object*, is common. Also, saying that sex with prostitutes is the best sex does not mean that more satisfying relationships do not exist in the future—after therapy.

Loneliness and feeling unloved are not addressed in the preceding quotation, but they are probably, at times, experienced.

The spiritual journey involves looking at why "bought" sex feels so good.

I'm moving away from thinking about right or wrong and considering what is healthy and unhealthy.

Dishonesty

I fake intimacy with my husband. I tell lies and often fake an orgasm. I realize that I am sexually dishonest.

A spouse can be dishonest in faking an orgasm and not be a sex addict. However, someone who continues to be dishonest concerning sexual enjoyment or sexual needs has a problem. It is certainly true that the spouse of a sex addict often fakes satisfaction because of the frequency of sex or the nature of what is requested sexually and pretends—codependently—to be happy and involved.

I've always believed that a component of spirituality is a willingness to share challenges in therapy, which can lead to recovery and healing. Sexual intimacy between alienated partners can take place—but a *program of action* must be embraced.

A spiritual word used in recovery circles is *surrender*: the willingness to accept what is not working and the humility to seek help.

My act of surrender involved seeing a therapist.

Education

What is healthy sex?

The answer to this question would probably involve writing a book. However, from my conversations over the years with sex therapists, I have learned the following:

- Healthy sex is doing or expressing yourself sexually in a way that brings sexual satisfaction to yourself and does not hurt or damage your partner.
- Healthy sex always involves the expression of honest feelings and emotions.
- There is no one way of expressing healthy sexuality. Healthy sexuality celebrates the variety and diversity of human expression and needs.
- Boundaries are always involved. Children must never be abused; a partner should never be forced; when someone wants to stop, those wishes must be respected.
- Spirituality involves an understanding of healthy sexuality.

Today I know that respect is the foundation for healthy sexual expression.

Exhibitionisn

I love people to watch me masturbate. Actually,
I love people to say good things about my body.
It's all about me.

As an alcoholic I often found myself disregarding and disrespecting the needs of others. It was all about what *I* thought, what *I* wanted to do, that *my* needs were being met. Spiritually, I was bankrupt.

A hidden insecurity that is rarely discussed is often at the core of low self-esteem, but it is covered by the addict's needs being met at the expense of loved ones and friends.

For many, this selfish behavior creates its own loneliness and despair, and the sex addict cries out for help. This addict's self-obsession created its own feelings of absolute emptiness. He asked for help.

Spirituality often involves owning the pain, sharing the guilt and shame, and confronting the symptoms of low self-esteem.

Whatever the situation, recovery is available.

Today I am willing to confront
the masks I hid behind.

Isolation

I don't let people get close. If a girlfriend starts to get close or to plan for the future, I drop her. I prefer being alone.

We often say something that we don't really mean. I heard the preceding quotation in a treatment center that treated sexual compulsivity. Although this client said, "I prefer being alone," he didn't. His loneliness had led to at least two suicide attempts. He didn't want to be alone, but he *feared intimacy.*

Spiritually, intimacy was the treatment for his sexual anorexia. He was a loner, he was isolated, and he wouldn't let people get close—because he did not feel good enough. His life was based on this thought: "If you got to know me you would not like me, and then you would leave me."

Over the months in treatment, I saw him becoming a positive and creative human being. He was able to maintain and grow a relationship. He found his spiritual foundation in Sex Addicts Anonymous (SAA).

Can a leopard change its spots? Yes, it can—*poetically!*

Today I will not say negative things about myself. I will seek to be positive.

Questions

I don't really enjoy sex. Am I asexual or a sexual anorexic?

I've always believed that life is complicated for most people. When we say, "I don't really enjoy sex," we may mean that we are not enjoying the type of sex we are experiencing. I've discovered that many people are ignorant of the variety of sexual experiences.

To understand the difference between someone who is asexual and someone who is a sexual anorexic would probably require a visit to a sex therapist or a really good sex information book. Nonetheless, it is undeniably true that some people are not interested in sex, do not have sexual drive or desires, and dislike physical contact—and they are to be respected.

However, it is still possible to be spiritually intimate and connected without physical expression. Celibates have lived this life in every generation. Indeed, celibacy is another aspect of love.

Today I respect and celebrate the different boundaries and needs of humankind.

Diversity

I'm in an open relationship. It's good for me and her. Is anything wrong with me?

It is important that we celebrate the variety and diversity of humankind, and this certainly includes relationships.

Whereas many different types of relationships can be found, most people feel comfortable and secure in a committed monogamous relationship. For religious people, this is called *marriage*.

Some people have an *open* relationship. If this works for the people concerned and it is based upon honest and clear communication, I have no right to be critical. However, I emphasize *honesty*.

Sex addiction and damaged relationships often begin with lies and manipulation, which are the enemies of spirituality. When dishonesty enters any relationship, sadness and pain usually follow. In the preceding quotation, we can celebrate the "open" relationship because it is "good for me and her."

My spiritual philosophy acknowledges the differences in human relationships.

Religious Abuse

Anything sexual seemed to be condemned by my church. Sex was a sin. Saints avoided sex. Is that why I'm a sexual anorexic?

A person exhibits the symptoms of sexual anorexia for many reasons. It is important to remember that the sexual anorexic is not necessarily someone who does not have sex; rather, it is the person who is unable to be intimate, who feels separate within the relationship.

From the many conversations I've had with sex addicts and sexual anorexics, it is clear that rigid religious messages that severely condemn masturbation, homosexuality, and sex outside of marriage play a pivotal role in fostering covert and secretive behaviors that can easily lead to sexual compulsivity.

The spiritual program embraces honesty and developing a life with beliefs and behaviors that are congruent. Sex Addicts Anonymous (SAA) has from its beginning stressed the need for rigorous honesty alongside a gentle willingness to confront covert and deceitful behavior.

God, I seek your love in the religious messages I hear.

Addiction Wars

Human beings fight many different kinds of war. My fight has been sex addiction. I believe sex addiction has killed many. I do not intend to be a victim.

We often hear the term *war on drugs*, and it is not unusual to hear the word *war* applied to sex addiction. The number of people affected by this sickness is incredible and includes addicts, families, and millions of others who are pulled into prostitution and pornography.

What are we to do? For many, and this might include you, the first step is knowing what is happening and how sex addiction creeps into many aspects of our lives and pleasures. Denial has long been an obstacle preventing people from realizing what is actually happening. Once we get honest, we are better able to focus on the best treatment and suggested recovery.

Today I am willing to talk about
my battle with sex addiction.

Fear of Intimacy

I've always been a loner, even when I was a child.
I've never been in love. However, I enjoy sex.
Usually I use the Internet or a magazine,
occasionally prostitutes.

The preceding quote encompasses a classic profile of a sexual anorexic: someone who is unable to be intimate or make an emotional relationship with his or her sexual partner.

The original break or separateness from family and friends often occurred in childhood. How? Why? Regardless of the many reasons, the affected person becomes a sexual loner.

Spirituality is always about connection: creating a healthy sexual relationship that enables the person to be present with a partner physically, mentally, and emotionally.

The 12 Step programs of Sex Addicts Anonymous (SAA) and Sex and Love Addicts Anonymous (SLAA) have proved invaluable. Let us not forget, though, that spiritual surrender might also include seeing a therapist or going into treatment.

The psalmist said, "Be still and know that
I am God." In my stillness, I asked for help.

Intimacy

I've described that I'm sexually compulsive when I'm with a girl, but when we separate I can easily forget her. I don't desire intimacy.

A spiritual component of intimacy is the ability to be emotionally connected. I've often said that the spiritual model for personal wellness—being mindful of our physical, mental, and emotional well-being—is also the key to a healthy relationship. *Real* intimacy has three components: a combination of the physical, mental, and emotional aspects of who we are as people. In the preceding quotation, we read that this individual is not involved mentally and emotionally: "I don't desire intimacy."

I remember hearing this information from a friend who attends Sex Addicts Anonymous (SAA). Although he said he didn't desire intimacy, he was attending meetings because his sex addiction had caused acute loneliness and depression. Surrender is letting go of pretense and embracing the reality of our emotional wounds.

Lord, today I appreciate the gift of intimacy.

Low Self-Esteem

I fear sexual rejection, so I don't seek a companion. Even as a young boy at school, I hated going into the showers with other boys. And I'm lonely.

The feeling of shame is related to issues of low self-esteem, of not feeling good enough. Being embarrassed about how we look can eventually lead to isolation and loneliness.

Spirituality, including developing a prayer life and times of silent meditation, also involves a love and respect for who we are—including our physical nature. It is difficult to be a positive and creative human being if you go through life fearing sexual rejection and feeling "less than."

A spiritual routine might include taking time to meet with a therapist who specializes in issues related to sexuality. Fear of intimacy and lack of self-esteem that foster lonely existence often form a background for sex addiction and sexual anorexia. From a spiritual perspective, help and recovery are available.

Today I'm willing to ask.

Sexual Anorexia

I have a panic attack when I'm asked to take off my clothes—even with my boyfriend. But I'm good at satisfying him. However, I never get my own needs met!

Romance addiction, or love addiction, is an aspect of codependency: feeling okay with ourselves if we are able to satisfy another. In the above quote, we also see the shame and low self-esteem expressed in the panic attacks related to being asked to remove clothing.

The spiritual program includes the support and healing required to establish self-esteem, self-love, and healthy boundaries. Nobody wants to suggest that we shouldn't care for others, but as Jesus taught, "Love your neighbor *as yourself*."

Many love addicts are getting support in Sex and Love Addicts Anonymous (SLAA), and not a few are seeking therapy.

Today love is a gift
I enthusiastically give to myself.

Boundaries

My family members want to attend Sex Addicts Anonymous (SAA) meetings with me, but I prefer to keep my meetings, and what is said, to myself. Am I selfish?

I don't think the person quoted here is selfish. I understand from my own experience that our recovery can be very personal and not something we want to share with family or close friends. Occasionally, my sister or a close friend has attended a recovery meeting with me, but most times I enjoy going alone to listen and share. I told the members of my family that this anonymity was important to me, that it was also spiritual, and they understood. Perhaps a similar conversation with this person's family is needed.

Family members can attend other "open" Sex Addicts Anonymous (SAA) meetings if they wish to understand more about the steps toward recovery.

My spiritual journey often embraces privacy.

Shyness

*I hate sex. I've not had sex for years, and I truly
don't miss it. I'm painfully shy.*

Some people are not sexual. The physical act of sex is
not something they need. Their sexuality is expressed
and manifested in other ways: service, writing, deep
friendships, and so on. In recovery we celebrate the spiritual diversity of humankind, and this includes the nonsexual.

I am concerned, however, with the sentiment
expressed in the preceding quotation: "I hate sex." Hate
is an extremely strong emotion and rarely has a role in
the living of the spiritual life. Rigid and judgmental religious teachings can often produce this negative reaction,
teaching that righteous and holy people avoid sex or can
do without it.

Spiritual healing requires a gentle exploration into the
source of these strong sentiments. Whether a person is
sexually active or not is his or her choice, but from a
spiritual perspective sex is always to be respected, never
hated.

Today I respect the gift of sexuality.

Ridicule

My brother forced me to have sex when I was young. He made fun of my small penis. Now I live alone, and I rarely have sex. Occasionally I will masturbate.

The roots of sexual dysfunction, especially sexual anorexia, which has often been described as the inability to create intimate relationships, starts, for many people, in childhood abuse: the cruel and violent things people, often family members, do to others. Here we have one brother abusing another.

Abuse happens, and it can have tragic consequences. Still, it is not the end of the story. Many people who were abused or who suffer from sexual anorexia are recovering, and they affirm a spiritual awakening in their lives.

The fact that it is difficult to talk about sexual issues does not mean that it is not happening. People realize that if they don't confront the abuse, then things will inevitably stay the same. In this sense, spirituality incorporates the theme of intervention.

Today I know that my spiritual awakening began when I asked for help.

Low Self-Worth

I love watching girls in strip clubs. Then I go home and masturbate.

An aspect of sex addiction involves voyeurism. For many people this involves the secretive use of pornography and the Internet, but many men and women seek out strip clubs.

Healthy sexuality, for most people, would require some level of intimacy: the sharing of feelings, the willingness to be vulnerable. Even in the crowded room of the strip club, the voyeur remains isolated, left only with his imaginings.

Spiritual healing begins with the creation of empowering affirmations:

- I am capable of change.
- I am lovable.
- I am ready to share my feelings with somebody I can trust.

These positive messages often provides the catalyst for changing our reality.

God, I am using your powerful spirit
in affirming my transformation.

Body Image

I'm a codependent. I'm fat. And my therapist thinks I might be a sexual anorexic. But I'm not sexual.

Some sexual anorexics do not have sex. They either do not have the urge for sex or their self-esteem is so low they feel that nobody would want to be with them. A powerful statement in the preceding quotation is, "I'm fat." Maybe this, alongside other experiences, sets up the separation and loneliness.

The spiritual journey is always about connection. The 12 Step program has opened the door to healing and recovery for many people with different addictions. It also introduces for some people the power of spirituality: being a positive and creative human being.

Maybe therapy—another aspect of spirituality—will also be required.

Today I understand that spirituality involves connection.

Unmanageable

I use people for sex. Sometimes I can have sex three or four times a day with different prostitutes. It is causing me financial problems. But I've never really had a girlfriend.

I cannot remember the age of the person who shared the preceding statement with me, but I do remember his profound sadness—especially when he said, "But I've never really had a girlfriend."

Most people are able to enjoy our lives because of the *special* relationships that we make. How sad to have only paid acquaintances!

The man quoted here was in therapy and was attending Sex Addicts Anonymous (SAA) meetings. How he had been living for years need not be the end of his story—recovery and healing are available.

I've described spirituality as the ingredient that helps us become positive and creative human beings. Our *essential* personalities are able to blossom, and we are able to establish special and loving relationships.

Today I am able to love and be loved.

Binge Sex

I binge on sex for months. I use the Internet, prostitutes, and porno magazines. Then I don't have sex for weeks. I've been like this for years. I don't really have any close friends.

I've known alcoholics and food addicts who binged for weeks and months, followed by bouts of abstinence and diets: sick cycles that consume a life! We often see a similar pattern in the sex addict.

The isolation is seen in the statement, "I don't really have any close friends."

My spiritual life is fed by my close friends. I enjoy my family, but I *need* my friends. Not only do they support and nurture me, but they also give me a perspective about who I am. When I was a drinking alcoholic, nobody really knew me, and so I can identify with the preceding quotation.

In recovery, we celebrate change. We affirm healing and the possibility of intimacy for those willing to ask for help. Recovery must be requested!

Thank you, God, for the discovered love in close friendships.

Disconnection

I got married when I was seventeen. We rarely have sex. I often think my husband and I are strangers. I love books. My husband watches television.

A loveless relationship is a tragedy. It is sad to live with someone and yet feel no connection. Unfortunately I've witnessed many such relationships.

Spirituality is never about settling. It does not celebrate mediocrity or absence of intimacy. Truly, spirituality is about love.

What do you do if you are in a loveless relationship? I suggest seeing a therapist. Years ago people felt that if you needed to see a therapist or, worse, a psychiatrist, you were crazy. I thank God that today such attitudes are expressed by a minority of the population. Many people are helped in their personal lives and relationships by social workers and therapists. Indeed, for me, therapy is an aspect of spiritual healing. To stay in an unhappy and loveless relationship is not a requirement for today's society.

I affirm love and intimacy
in my relationships.

Religious Codependency

You wrote in Say Yes to Your Life *that God is not a bellboy. What did you mean?*

We are sometimes given, in probably all religions, the message that if we ask God for something, call Him up with a prayerful request, then He will deliver. That's a little like calling the front desk of a five-star hotel and getting a delivery from the bellboy.

I'm more inclined to the spiritual position that affirms our involvement with whatever we want to happen in our lives. As a recovering alcoholic I truly believe that God *wanted* me sober but didn't *make* me get sober. I needed to seek help and attend support groups, and this is my view regarding sex addiction. The people who are in recovery are the people who did something, made the changes, sought the therapy, and attended support groups.

In recovery, you get something when you *do* something.

*I pray and move my feet in the
direction of the prayer.*

Thanksgiving

I give thanks for my recovery from sex addiction. It's much more important than a turkey or pumpkin pie.

When I have the Thanksgiving feast at my home, I always remember my friends who are in recovery. I thank God for the gift of the 12 Step program that I've now embraced for many years, and it has brought me healing and strength beyond my best imaginings. I thank God for the people who enter treatment and therapy, fearing their future but trusting the hope that family and friends have conveyed to them. I thank God for the friends and families of addicts who walked through the pain with them and now are enjoying the recovery.

Thanksgiving is a time of remembered healing, and occasionally I feel sorry for the turkey!

Thank you for this miracle called recovery.

Therapy

I'm sixty years old, and I've never been married. I've had a few girlfriends, but the sex was not good. I suppose I'm shy, but I'm a compulsive masturbator. Do I need help?

It is not easy to decide who needs help. When it comes to the topic of addiction, most professionals suggest that only the individuals facing the challenges can decide if they need help. A concern expressed in the preceding quotation is, "But I'm a compulsive masturbator." One aspect of sex addiction is compulsive behavior.

Occasionally I've heard people say, "Why worry?" if someone is elderly. "Let them enjoy themselves." However, such sentiments are off base. A person at sixty-six can still be in emotional pain. Regardless of age, everyone has the right to health and happiness.

It might be helpful to see a therapist or attend a Sex Addicts Anonymous (SAA) meeting. It's a great feeling to know that you are not alone with a problem and to see that people are making healthy changes in their lives.

Great Spirit, I'm old enough to feel young.

Recovery

Once sexual anorexia was explained, I began to understand myself. I've been in recovery for four years.

Knowledge is power. When we understand what a term or phrase means, we are better able to see if it applies to our thinking and behavior. *Sexual anorexia*, for many people, is a confusing expression because at first glance you might think it means *not having sex*. However, the description is about a lack or absence of sexual intimacy, being unable to express feelings, or a fear of being known. Sexual anorexics are usually lonely, with extreme feelings of isolation, but they can still be sexual.

In the preceding quotation, we hear from a person who first was able to identify with a sexual condition and then was able to embrace recovery.

I had a similar experience with alcoholism. When I heard some symptoms explained to me, I was able to admit and accept my alcoholism. Knowledge, or information, is power!

God, only when I know myself
can I truly love myself.

Spiritual Laws

I'm reading about the spiritual Law of Attraction. Did I bring sex addiction into my life?

The spiritual Law of Attraction—*what we think, what we say, what we envision, we can create in our lives*—is popular these days. It speaks of living a focused life: a life of intention.

However, most teachers of this spiritual law would not suggest that we bring diseases or calamities *intentionally* but that we can utilize the Law of Attraction to affirm healing and recovery.

We affirm honesty. We see our family growing together in recovery. We make the intention of personal healing. One day at a time.

*Today I am envisioning
happiness and healing.*

Confusion

Is a sex addict a person who really enjoys sex?

It is true that some sex addicts find sex so pleasurable and euphoric that they cannot stop thinking about it. They cannot stop wanting to engage in all manner of sexual activity, but it rarely stays that way. The combination of secrecy, dishonesty, shame, and fear of being found out usually all combine to create sadness, depression, and possibly suicidal feelings.

Other sex addicts say that although they are abusive and compulsive about sex, they don't really enjoy it. The guilt and shame destroy any feelings of enjoyment. From the very beginning, they say, they felt "dirty."

Sex addiction, like other addictions, is cunning, baffling, and powerful, and it affects people differently, producing different feelings and responses.

*I accept the complexity of
my sexual feelings.*

Gratitude

I took responsibility for my sex addiction two years ago. Now I'm in recovery. I'm able to be intimate with my wife. I'm able to share with my children. Life is good.

The message here is "I am affirming wellness, recovery, and the healing of relationships."

It is important for people to know, because many people do relapse and return to sexual compulsivity, that there are men and women enjoying a spiritual recovery. "Life is good."

The more people are given information, made aware of therapy and treatment, and familiarize themselves with the growing number of 12 Step support groups, the more people will discover and enjoy recovery for sex addiction.

A key challenge to be faced lies in the shame and secrecy that surround most things sexual in our society. Because of positive information and healthy publicity, this stigma is beginning to be addressed.

My spiritual healing helped
to heal my family.

December

Confusion

How can a sexual addiction be unhealthy?
I'm proud of my sexual energy.

Let me be clear: I'm not judging or condemning a healthy sexual energy. I believe that sex is a gift from God and when expressed in a healthy manner, is a key ingredient for romance and intimacy.

But sexual addiction is about a lack of balance, compulsive sexual behaviors that create feelings of *powerlessness,* and *unmanageable* behaviors.

Today I do not confuse sexual addiction with a healthy and active sexual expression.

God, I thank you for the gift of sexual energy
which I express responsibly.

Question

Did God make me a sex addict?

I really don't think that God *makes* us anything. I'm much more inclined toward the spiritual concept of co-creation: that we partner with God in creating our lives. However, I do believe that our family of origin and environment can play an important part in *influencing* our attitudes and behaviors.

Spirituality involves knowing that we have the power to be positive and creative human beings regardless of the challenges that life presents. It's interesting to discuss why and how a person became a sex addict, but the real question is, "What are we going to do about it?" I suggest that a person attend Sex Addicts Anonymous (SAA) meetings and also consider seeing a therapist or getting treatment.

People are recovering from sex addiction, and individual lives and relationships are being healed.

*Today I seek to live
in the solution.*

Ignorance

To my friends I laughed about my sex addiction,
but inside I cried. I was spiritually bankrupt.

I know this feeling. When I was drinking I often felt empty, lost, ashamed, disgusted—and bankrupt.

Many addicts have described themselves as "walking zombies," the "living dead," drifting "phantoms," but the description in the 12 Step program fits perfectly: *We were spiritually bankrupt.*

I feel that the sex addict sinks a bit deeper than most other addicts because of the religious shame and indescribable guilt that sex addicts carry in our society. True, we often laugh about sex, but behind "the mask" are fear and shame.

The antidote to this utter despair is recovery, either in Sex Addicts Anonymous (SAA) or some other 12 Step program, therapy, or treatment. Let's face it, prayer without action has proven for many to be useless.

Today I know I have the divine power
to heal my spiritual bankruptcy.

Spirituality

I've never gone to church, but I think I'm spiritual. Can you be spiritual and not practice a religion?

Absolutely! Some people, who could never experience God in a church or synagogue, are able to find God in nature, art, music, and poetry. It is also possible to be both spiritual and religious. Tragically, we occasionally meet the fanatic who is obsessively religious but not spiritual!

A helpful definition of spirituality, especially for recovering people, and this includes the sex addict, is having a *positive* attitude and developing *creative* behaviors. This is helpful because often the addict has felt extremely negative about himself or herself and certainly engaged in destructive behaviors, usually for years.

Yes, I'm discovering more and more people who describe themselves as spiritual but are not involved in any religion.

*Today my spirituality is fed
by my support meetings.*

Surrender

I hear the word surrender at meetings, but I think it really reinforces that I have a weakness.

Many people have a problem with the word *surrender* for the exact reason expressed in the preceding quotation: *It really reinforces that I have a weakness.*

I do not have a problem with the word *surrender*. I consider that a person surrenders because he or she does not want to die and surrenders to live. In this sense, *surrender* is a very powerful word.

In the context of my recovery from alcoholism, I believe I surrendered to the realization that if I continued to drink I would continue to have problems. I raised the white handkerchief (metaphorically speaking) and decided that I would get help for my alcoholism. I did not want to continue the battle. I did not want to die.

Today I continue to surrender to this belief, *one day at a time.*

Spiritually,
I surrender to live.

Amends

I'm making my amends for my sexually addictive past, and it is going well. People are so kind and understanding. Honesty really is the best policy.

Sometimes our expectations about what is going to happen bear no resemblance to the reality. I remember a quote from Winston Churchill that said something like, "Most of the thoughts that kept me awake at night never happened."

Addicts live with fear, even in the early stages of recovery. Making amends, saying "Sorry," apologizing for past behaviors are never easy, and I can only imagine the anxiety this might provoke for the sex addict. Yet, as I discovered when I made amends for my alcoholic escapades, people are often really kind and understanding. They are mostly pleased to know that you are taking responsibility for your addiction, getting help, and receiving support. I've discovered that friendships are recovered and maintained on a deeper level.

Honesty is a spiritual policy.

Denial

*My wife is a sex addict, but we can't discuss it.
I'm really worried, but I pretend nothing
is happening.*

Codependency—an unwillingness to face reality, a *severe denial* that has been described as an elephant in the living room that nobody is willing to acknowledge—is common with families and friends of addicts. Sex addiction often remains secretive because of a rigid religious morality and a society that is largely uncomfortable discussing all things sexual. This background feeds the denial not only in the sex addict but also in family members.

Intervention is a therapeutic technique for helping the family. A knowledgeable professional will meet privately with family members and arrange a safe and spiritual confrontation, *based on love and respect*, concerning unacceptable behavior.

Yes, family members and addicts are getting help, experiencing lasting recovery.

*Lord, I'm discovering the
courage to face my fears.*

Recovery

*The spiritual program in Sex Addicts
Anonymous has changed my life. Everything
has improved.*

In my recovery from alcoholism, I cannot emphasize enough my gratitude to the support program that has saved my life and given me purpose. Included in my gratitude are the medical and psychiatric treatments I received and the period of time I spent in a sober living home.

In sobriety I came to America. I've written numerous books and appeared on a major television talk show. That's not shabby for a drunken alcoholic who some years ago wanted to die! Today I can fully appreciate the spirit of the preceding quotation: "Everything has improved."

*Today I seek to live an
attitude of gratitude.*

Love Addiction

A friend, who like me is recovering from alcoholism, says that I'm a love addict. Is that like being codependent?

Codependency and love addiction are somewhat similar, in that both express a neediness. However, whereas codependency can involve any aspect of relationship, the love addict specifically relates to romance: a neediness for love. Yet, because of their neediness, love addicts stay in relationships that combine physical, mental, and emotional abuse.

Developing a spiritual respect and love of self are essential for recovery. One powerful support group is Sex and Love Addicts Anonymous (SLAA). Another is COSA, which is the Al-Anon for family and friends of sex addicts.

In the preceding quotation, the addict reveals that a friend "says . . . I'm a love addict." Indeed, the addict may see something that supports this observation, but it would probably be more helpful and informative to see a professional who treats love addiction.

*Today I am open to information that
helps me understand who I am.*

Acceptance

I feared telling my parents that I've been treated for sex addiction. But they accepted me.

Spirituality involves not only a respect for other people but also an acceptance: an acceptance that affirms that people are different, with a variety of qualities and challenges. This diversity includes the sex addict.

I'm a recovering alcoholic. My parents accepted me: indeed, they often attended support programs with me. My mother had a congenitally weak heart, my father had diabetes, and I was an alcoholic. Different sicknesses, different challenges—all were accepted by family and friends.

A fear regarding sex addiction is the guilt, shame, and variety of religious taboos. Slowly they are being overcome, and people are being accepted.

Love involves acceptance—
but not, necessarily, agreement.

Ongoing Recovery

*My sex addiction seems to be going away now
that I'm in recovery for my alcoholism.*

It is certainly true that if a person gets involved in a recovery program for alcoholism, especially if that program incorporates the 12 Steps, he or she has a spiritual foundation for healing. Most recovery programs emphasize personal responsibility, discovering God or Higher Power, a willingness to examine what must change, making amends where appropriate, and a continuing focus on maintaining spiritual health.

However, I'm not convinced that a recovery program for alcoholism speaks directly to the issues of sex addiction. Friends of mine who have a sex addiction alongside alcoholism find it helpful to attend a support program for each addiction. From a spiritual perspective, it is more comfortable to attend a support program that involves your own peers.

*I'm discovering myself in
the sharing of others.*

Hope

Is sex addiction like being a pedophile: there is no cure?

In the treatment of addiction the word *cure* is not used, but healing and recovery certainly are to be had. This is true for the pedophile and other sex addicts.

The more psychologists, psychiatrists, and therapists treat these sicknesses and understand more about the physiological makeup and background of these addictions, the greater the success.

In recovery we say, "We are as sick as our secrets." Therefore, a key component of treatment is the mental health workers who create the bridge to healing. Their insights, acceptance, understanding, and the respect they show each patient will create trust and self-disclosure.

Spirituality heals the wounded. The mental health worker often has been wounded in the past, and this empathy creates the connection with the addict.

In the challenges of others,
I recognize my own woundedness.

Fantasy

I married a man but never told him I was a sex addict. Now I'm fantasizing about having sex with his four brothers.

"Honesty is the best policy" has become a cliché around the world because, spiritually speaking, it rings true. It is also true that tragedy follows dishonesty.

If we lie or keep important secrets from the person we love, then problems will surely follow. In the preceding quotation, we see how secret sexual fantasizing involves family members.

Denial or covert behavior is never the answer for addiction, and there is no magic bullet. What leads to spiritual healing and recovery is honest communication, possibly therapy or treatment—and yes, ongoing support programs.

"That's too much," some people say. But look at the gains: honest relationships, healthy boundaries, and a respect of self.

My spiritual program often involves facing inconvenient truths.

Therapy

*I believe my husband is sexually compulsive.
It has now progressed into a serious addiction.
What should I do?*

Years ago I was a heavy drinker. Then I crossed the line. It's hard for me to put my finger on the exact day or month, but I crossed the line into alcoholism. Addiction professionals tell us that addiction is a *progressive disease*. It appears that the husband mentioned in the preceding quotation has crossed the line into sex addiction.

This point of no return can now lead to recovery, a healing of anxiety for the wife, and the possibility of a blessed marriage. The spiritual program that could bring healing in this marriage will probably require therapy alongside attendance at Sex Addicts Anonymous (SAA) support groups.

The wife can also heal in COSA, the Al-Anon of SAA for family and friends.

*Recovery is not free. It requires an
ongoing commitment to change.*

Surrender

*I know I'm a sex addict. Do I need to see
a therapist?*

Not every sex addict needs therapy; however most, if
not all, are usually helped by seeing a therapist. I
think that therapy is an aspect of spirituality because it
involves the healing of painful memories, along with a
deeper awareness of family dynamics and the addict's
role in developing his or her personality. It also offers
insights into how we can create happiness in our lives.

However, I've met people who were healed and trans-
formed in Sex Addicts Anonymous (SAA) support
meetings. They applied themselves to the 12 Step program, selected and used a sponsor, and experienced the
promised spiritual awakening.

I suggest that the person cited in the preceding quotation attend Sex Addicts Anonymous (SAA) meetings.
If the sexual compulsivity continues, the addict should
seek out a therapist.

*Today my affirmation is not to do
anything but to do something.*

Religious Co-Dependency

Religion did not seem to help me heal from my
sex addiction. Maybe it will in the future.
Today I need therapy.

I've heard this sentiment often, and it usually reflects an idea of religion, or God, that expects a magical answer to prayer. For example:

- God, please take away my sexual compulsivity.
- God, remove my impure thoughts that concern children.
- God, make me a better husband and father.

These prayers are religiously codependent. They are expecting God to fix, remove, or stop certain attitudes and behaviors.

The spiritual theme I offer is co-creation: that God has given us the ability to change our behaviors, heal our destructive thinking, and create recovery.

We can rarely do this alone. Most of us must ask for help, seeking therapy and, possibly, treatment.

I'm discovering a God who is
involved in my decisions.

Recovery

I really enjoy going to my Sex Addicts Anonymous
meetings. I never really understood spirituality
until I went to these support groups.

My attendance at support groups for recovering alcoholics gave me my first real introduction into spirituality, and I was an Episcopalian priest! I've since become a Unity minister.

Today I can find God in a church, synagogue, mosque, or temple, but I can also find my Higher Power in recovery groups, nature, loving relationships, life's challenges, nature, art, music, and poetry.

For years I had made God a prisoner of my church, my religion, but now I am able to experience God in a myriad of experiences and situations.

Today my God is an expansive
spiritual experience.

12 Step

*I'm a sex addict, and I thank God for the
12 Step program.*

I think it is important to acknowledge the healing and transformational energy that many have discovered in the 12 Step program, which was created by a group of suffering alcoholics in the United States. These brave men and women discovered healing and recovery by sharing their thoughts, challenges, and concerns with each other.

This concept has now been developed and applied to millions suffering from a variety of addictions, including sex addiction.

Can you recover without the 12 Steps? Yes, but most addicts need the support, advice, and camaraderie of people who have faced similar challenges. The spiritual component, which is the foundation of any 12 Step program, also emphasizes the need to review and possibly change all areas of our life. In this sense it is truly comprehensive and transformative.

*The 12 Step program celebrates
ordinary miracles.*

Healing

My therapist suggests that I embrace my sex addiction, hold it close to my heart. Only then will the healing begin.

One component of spirituality is our willingness to face our challenges, as well as to embrace them because they are part of who we are.

I've heard many therapists suggest to people with a food addiction that they entertain the idea of *loving* food—it is *not* the enemy. Only when we are able to love a gift from God are we able to respect it and then enter the process of healing.

I think this is true for sex addiction. It is our abuse and misuse of sex that is the challenge—not sexuality itself. When we release the healing energy of love, we open ourselves to the possibility of change and recovery.

Today I understand that
loving myself involves a love and
respect for my addiction.

Prosperity

*Can you believe that five years ago I was
bankrupt because of my sex addiction? Today
I'm in recovery with money in the bank.*

There is a saying in 12 Step communities: "It just keeps getting better," and this includes finances.

The foundation of healing is spiritual. Is money spiritual? Absolutely. For many it is the key to freedom.

The freedom to live involves money. Food, health, travel, education, housing, support for family and friends—all involve money. Indeed, it is impossible to live *without any money.*

Addiction inevitably affects our personal wealth, often creating financial insecurity and, possibly, poverty. It is expensive to feed an addiction. Drugs, alcohol, sex, romance—they don't come cheap.

Like the sex addict in the preceding quotation, I became financially solvent when I got sober. And then I discovered the beauty of life in God's world.

*Today I respect the spiritual energy
that is created by money.*

Responsibility

God accepts me. God forgives me. But I must take responsibility for my life.

An aspect of religious abuse often involves *magical thinking*—that is, the idea that God will remove any obstacle in our lives without our involvement.

Let me be clear: I do believe in miracles, but I do believe that possibly the greatest miracle is our ability to involve ourselves in creating a better and healthier life for ourselves. Regarding addiction, recovery is dependent upon our willingness to change unhealthy behaviors and seek help.

In the preceding quotation we read, "God accepts me. God forgives me." This is true, yet the real healing begins when we are able to accept and love ourselves.

Recovery celebrates the miracle of our being able to respond positively to any challenge.

I understand and accept the spiritual dynamic of responsibility.

Al-Anon

As the wife of a sex addict, I realize it was the spirituality I found in Al-Anon that kept me sane.

When we discuss sex addiction, it is important not to forget the families and relationships that are affected by this *cunning, baffling, and powerful disease.* Many families and friends can no longer live with the progressive madness and feel a need to walk away. Yet many remain.

Al-Anon and COSA (the Al-Anon of Sex Addicts Anonymous for families and friends) provide continuing support and a spiritual foundation for family members and friends of sex addicts.

Family members live with symptoms similar to those that are experienced by the sex addict: guilt, shame, fear, confusion, and personal self-loathing. They often blame themselves, and they desperately need a safe place to express their feelings.

Al-Anon groups and COSA provide such a place.

I'm grateful for the serenity I've discovered at my Al-Anon meetings.

Fear

My wife left me, even though she said she still loved me. Why did she leave me? Because she could not take my use of pornography any longer. She was afraid for the children.

Before I got sober my mother sat with me in the kitchen and said, "Leo, I love you enough to let you go. I'm letting you go not because I've ceased to love you, but *because I love you.*" Soon after this intervention I got sober.

We see a similar incident in the preceding quotation: the tragedy of a wife walking away from the husband she still loved because of his use of pornography and its effects upon family life.

Sex addiction, like any addiction, affects and destroys relationships if it is left untreated.

The healing comes when we ask for help, seek therapy, and enter recovery.

Some people exclaim, "That's hard to do!" Is it really harder than losing your family?

Surrender, for me,
means asking for help.

Confusion

My sexual compulsivity made me into Jekyll and Hyde.

A friend of mine, who is an active sex addict, shared with me recently that he was living two lives. He had a family life that involved attendance at a Baptist church where he was an active member and a "secret life" that involved Internet pornography and prostitutes. The two lives were completely separate: Jekyll and Hyde!

Then I reflected on my own drinking years. I lived the life of an Episcopal priest by day and then became the drunk in the evening. My church congregation was surprised when I entered treatment—some didn't know that I drank! The two lives were separate: Jekyll and Hyde!

My healing came when I entered treatment. I confronted the denial and faced reality. In the process of my recovery, I experienced a "spiritual awakening" and I became *whole*.

Lord, I seek the peace that involves becoming an integrated human being.

Hope

Rudolph, the red-nosed reindeer
had a very shiny nose.
And if you ever saw him,
you would even say it glows.
All of the other reindeer
used to laugh and call him names.
They never let poor Rudolph
join in any reindeer games.

—*Johnny Mercer and Robert L. May*

As a recovering alcoholic, I feel for Rudolph; the red-nosed reindeer always made me tearfully proud. Rudolph was about me.

I think that sex addicts can identify: the cruel names that were used, the tittering mixed with sarcastic laughter, the feelings of isolation.

Then "the voice," the intervention, words of encouragement that conveyed hope—"I can move up to the front, move away from the despair, lead others if I embrace recovery."

Now people love me.

I seek to convey to others the hope
that Rudolph gave to me.

Courage

*Only when I entered recovery for my alcoholism
could I find the courage to face my sex addiction.*

Relapse—returning to past destructive behaviors—
often occurs through an untreated, prime addiction:
a drug addict who wishes to cling to his or her alcohol
use; a codependent who is unwilling to confront a love
addiction; and in the preceding quotation, we see an
alcoholic facing sex addiction.

This is spiritual progress. Years ago nobody talked
about or treated sex addiction. As Dr. Patrick Carnes has
reminded us, "It existed in the shadows."

Today more and more addicts are confronting their
sex addiction, avoiding future relapses, and enjoying a
complete spiritual recovery. No more deception, no more
manipulation, and the guilt and shame subside.

*Today I am willing to face and heal
the addictions in my life.*

Sponsorship

My therapist says I need a sponsor, but I go to meetings regularly.

With counseling sex addicts and alcoholics, I have often suggested that it might be helpful to get a sponsor. A sponsor is not a counselor and does not do therapy. A sponsor's role in recovery is to *be present*, to offer support concerning the application of the 12 Step program, and to give helpful advice concerning recovery issues.

Attending support meetings is great. Listening and sharing are important parts of the recovery process, but occasionally an addict must meet personally with another recovering person who has had more years of experience in the practice of the 12 Step program.

The sponsor is usually selected by the individual, who says, "I want what you have." The sponsor need not be a friend.

My sponsor is my spiritual lifeline.

Spirituality

Spirituality is the key to my sexual healing.

I describe spirituality as being a positive and creative human being. I distinguish spirituality from religion, which is an organization or denomination based upon certain historical beliefs, whereas spirituality is more comprehensive, including nature, art, music, and poetry.

I also suggest that spirituality involves how we love and nurture ourselves. This includes the continuing care of our body, mind, and feelings.

Addiction creates spiritual brokenness. It attacks the body, confuses the mind, and numbs our feelings. Sex addiction is no exception.

The recovery that is being experienced by more than a million people in this world affirms the preceding quotation: *Spirituality is the key to healing.*

*I am grateful for the healing experienced
in my spiritual journey.*

Gratitude

I've been in recovery from sexual addiction for five years. Today I take my message to treatment centers, schools, and churches. I'm taking a negative in my life and making it positive.

I've done the same with my alcoholism. It is powerful to share with other people, especially those who may be touched by the addiction but are too ashamed to admit it, the healing joy that comes with recovery. To hear the message of hope, to see a person honestly sharing what it was like, what happened, and what it is like now.

In recent years I've come to believe that recovery from addiction is the healing of the "new leprosy" in our society. The shame is replaced by a shared spiritual awakening.

Today, I willingly share what I gratefully received.

Financial Devastation

All my spare cash went to my sex addiction.

I heard a patient at a treatment center make the preceding statement. I remember asking, "Was it only your *spare* cash?"

He thought for a moment. "No. Now that I think about it, the money went from everywhere. It was like a gambling addiction!" In the 12 Step program, we hear that addiction is "cunning, baffling, and powerful." It is also expensive: hundreds of dollars—thousands of dollars—and the *cost* to a person's integrity.

But people do not have to stay lost in addiction. They do not have to drown in the shame of sex addiction. Thousands of men and women are in recovery.

First you must admit that you have a problem. This is the beginning of a spiritual journey that will lead to health and prosperity.

In recovery, my life is rich beyond my wildest dreams.

Gratitude

Today is the last day of the year. I didn't think I'd be in a treatment center for sex addiction. And I'm grateful.

I've been with many people who spent New Year's Eve in a treatment center. They exhibited a willingness to let go of what they wanted so that they could embrace what they needed—all in a safe place. That's surrender!

After a year of pain and confusion, it is wonderful to feel ordinarily *safe*—from yourself.

The last night of the year spent with a family of recovering people preparing for a new day—a New Year . . .

I've discovered it is the small things in life that really make me happy, and feeling safe is important.

Spiritually, I know that if I do not feel safe I will never be happy.

About the Author

Leo Booth, a former Episcopal Priest, is a Unity Minister; he is also a recovering alcoholic. At the end of many years of heavy drinking, he was in a horrific car crash. That moment made him realize that life is too important to waste and so he checked himself into a treatment center.

Leo was born in England and came to America in 1981. Because of his personal experience about the dangers of alcohol and drug abuse, he dedicated his work toward recovery. His passion for helping other recovering alcoholics and drug addicts inspired him to write his first book called *Say Yes to Life*. This book has helped thousands of people over the years.

Leo continues his involvement with counseling alcoholics and addicts in several treatment centers. He speaks at many drug and alcohol abuse conferences, mental health organizations, correctional facilities, and at churches throughout the country. His books include *Say Yes to Your Spirit* and *Say Yes to Your Life*.

Leo has appeared on such national television shows as *Oprah, Good Morning America,* and others. His articles appear in several recovery and health publications.

For more information about Leo Booth and his speaking engagements, visit: www.fatherleo.com. E-mail: fatherleo @fatherleo.com.